The Essentia

CITROËN
DS & ID
All models
1966 to 1975

Your marque expert: Rudy A Heilig

)

VELOCE PUBLISHING
THE PUBLISHER OF FINE AUTOMOTIVE BOOKS

Essential Buyer's Guide Series
Alfa GT (Booker)
Alfa Romeo Spider Giulia (Booker & Talbott)
Audi TT (Davies)
Austin Seven (Barker)
Big Healeys (Trummel)
BMW E21 3 Series (1975-1983) (Reverente, Cook)
BMW GS (Henshaw)
BMW X5 (Saunders)
BSA 500 & 650 Twins (Henshaw)
BSA Bantam (Henshaw)
Citroën 2CV (Paxton)
Citroën ID & DS (Heilig)
Cobra Replicas (Ayre)
Corvette C2 Sting Ray 1963-1967 (Falconer)
Ducati Bevel Twins (Falloon)
Ducati Desmodue Twins (Falloon)
Ducati Desmoquattro Twins (Falloon)
Fiat 500 & 600 (Bobbitt)
Ford Capri (Paxton)
Ford Escort Mk1 & Mk2 (Williamson)
Ford Mustang (Cook)
Ford RS Cosworth Sierra & Escort (Williamson)
Harley-Davidson Big Twins (Henshaw)
Hinckley Triumph triples & fours 750, 900, 955, 1000,
1050, 1200 – 1991-2009 (Henshaw)
Honda CBR600 Hurricane (Henshaw)
Honda CBR FireBlade (Henshaw)
Honda SOHC fours 1969-1984 (Henshaw)
Jaguar E-type 3.8 & 4.2-litre (Crespin)
Jaguar E-type V12 5.3-litre (Crespin)
Jaguar XJ 1995-2003 (Crespin)
Jaguar XK8 & XKR (1996-2005) (Thorley)
Jaguar/Daimler XJ6, XJ12 & Sovereign (Crespin)
Jaguar/Daimler XJ40 (Crespin)
Jaguar Mark 1 & 2 (All models including Daimler 2.5-litre
V8) 1955 to 1969 (Thorley)
Jaguar S-type – 1999 to 2007 (Thorley)
Jaguar X-type – 2001 to 2009 (Thorley)
Jaguar XJ-S (Crespin)
Jaugar XJ6, XJ8 & XJR (Thorley)
Jaguar XK 120, 140 & 150 (Thorley)

Kawasaki Z1 & Z900 (Orritt)
Land Rover Series I, II & IIA (Thurman)
Land Rover Series III (Thurman)
Lotus Seven replicas & Caterham 7: 1973-2013 (Hawkins)
Mazda MX-5 Miata (Mk1 1989-97 & Mk2 98-2001) (Crook)
Mercedes-Benz 280SL-560DSL Roadsters (Bass)
Mercedes-Benz 'Pagoda' 230SL, 250SL & 280SL
MGA 1955-1962 (Sear, Crosier)
MGF & MG TF (Hawkins)
MGB & MGB GT (Williams)
MG Midget & A-H Sprite (Horler)
MG TD, TF & TF1500 (Jones)
Mini (Paxton)
Morris Minor & 1000 (Newell)
New Mini (Collins)
Norton Commando (Henshaw)
Peugeot 205 GTI (Blackburn)
Porsche 911 (930) Turbo series (Streather)
Porsche 911 (964) (Streather)
Porsche 911 (993) (Streather)
Porsche 911 (996) (Streather)
Porsche 911 Carrera 3.2 series 1984 to 1989 (Streather)
Porsche 911SC – Coupé, Targa, Cabriolet & RS Model
years 1978-1983 (Streather)
Porsche 924 – All models 1976 to 1988 (Hodgkins)
Porsche 928 (Hemmings)
Porsche 930 Turbo & 911 (930) Turbo (Streather)
Porsche 944(Higgins, Mitchell)
Porsche 986 Boxster series (Streather)
Porsche 987 Boxster and Cayman series (Streather)
Rolls-Royce Silver Shadow & Bentley T-Series (Bobbitt)
Subaru Impreza (Hobbs)
Triumph Bonneville (Henshaw)
Triumph Stag (Mort & Fox)
Triumph TR7 & TR8 (Williams)
Triumph Thunderbird, Trophy & Tiger (Henshaw)
Vespa Scooters – Classic two-stroke models 1960-2008
(Paxton)
Volvo 700/900 Series (Beavis)
VW Beetle (Cservenka & Copping)
VW Bus (Cservenka & Copping)
VW Golf GTI (Cservenka & Copping)

www.veloce.co.uk

For post publication news, updates and amendments relating to this book please visit www.veloce.co.uk/book/V4138

First published in February 2008. Reprinted January 2014 by Veloce Publishing Limited, Veloce House, Parkway Farm Business Park, Middle Farm Way, Poundbury, Dorchester, Dorset, DT1 3AR, England.
Fax 01305 250479/e-mail info@veloce.co.uk/web www.veloce.co.uk or www.velocebooks.com.
ISBN: 978-1-84584-138-8 UPC: 6-36847-04138-0

© Rudy A Heilig and Veloce Publishing 2008 & 2014. All rights reserved. With the exception of quoting brief passages for the purpose of review, no part of this publication may be recorded, reproduced or transmitted by any means, including photocopying, without the written permission of Veloce Publishing Ltd. Throughout this book logos, model names and designations, etc, have been used for the purposes of identification, illustration and decoration. Such names are the property of the trademark holder as this is not an official publication.
Readers with ideas for automotive books, or books on other transport or related hobby subjects, are invited to write to the editorial director of Veloce Publishing at the above address.
British Library Cataloguing in Publication Data – A catalogue record for this book is available from the British Library.
Typesetting, design and page make-up all by Veloce Publishing Ltd on Apple Mac. Printed in India by Imprint Digital.

Introduction & thanks
– the purpose of this book

Introduction

In 1955, at the Paris Salon, the Citroën DS19 – arguably the most technologically innovative production car ever – was unveiled to the world. Never before had a single model embraced so many advances – it was revolutionary, not just in its unusual aerodynamic shape, but in its incredible leap in technology, placing the car ten to twenty years ahead of its contemporaries. Chief among the innovations was the hydraulic system that powered the adjustable self-levelling suspension, inboard disc brakes, rack-and-pinion steering and gear shifting. When added to Citroën's trademark front-wheel-drive, suspension, handling and wind-cheating shark-like body, the DS19 seemed like a futuristic spaceship in a world of horse-and-carts.

Over its 20-year life, the D-model was refined and improved, and the range was extended to include several variations including lower-tech 'intro level' models, cavernous Wagons, high-spec luxury versions and even ultra-exclusive coach-built Coupés and cabriolets. Due to its lengthy lifespan and numerous variations, this book is restricted to the 1966-1975 'Series 2' range of the D-model and does not delve deeply into the rare Chapron versions of the car. Fortunately, the Chapron-built cars are technically identical to the rest of the D variations and, if you are lucky enough to find a Chapron, this book will certainly help in your inspection and evaluation.

Although no book, no matter how detailed, can be a substitute for an in-depth inspection from a specialist, this one should help you weed out the 'junk' and narrow your search. Use this book wisely and it will provide inspection cost savings, bargaining power and an informed decision.

Thanks

This book was possible only through the help of family members and several D enthusiasts. Foremost, I am grateful for the 60 years of Citroën experience from my father, Hank Heilig, and the technical wizardry and critical eye from my brother, Paul Heilig, both whom provided the accuracy and knowledge required for this book. Special thanks are due to Wally Escherich, a well-known American Citroën enthusiast, who was always supportive and helpful in obtaining photos and material, and Citroën owner Michel Boucher

Author Rudy Heilig with his 1971 Citroën DS21.

whose continual support and helpful suggestions kept me going during trying times. Finally, I want to thank my wife Kelly and kids, Cassidy and Katie, who endured my late hours in front of the computer and absence from their activities.

Contents

Essential Buyer's Guide™ currency

At the time of publication a BG unit of currency "⬤" equals approximately £1.00/
US $1.62/Euro 1.20. Please adjust to suit current exchange rates.

Tall and short drivers

The D-model's cabin is incredibly roomy and comfortable – small wonder that it was the car of choice for the French government for almost 20 years. The seats don't have much lateral support but are almost sofa-like in comfort. Headroom is plentiful – even the back seat can accommodate all but the tallest passengers. The steering wheel is not adjustable but correctly placed with fingertip access to most switches. The flat, tunnel-free floor has ample legroom.

The suspension level in its highest position.

Weight of controls

Most D-models are equipped with hydraulically-assisted steering racks, making tight parking very manageable. Some ID19 models have manual non-assisted steering, demanding Herculean effort for car park manoeuvres. The D-model's hydraulic brakes are incredibly responsive as they don't need much foot pressure to bring the car to a screeching halt. The Citromatic gear change (four manually-shifted forward gears but no clutch pedal) also might take some getting used to. A forward shift comprises lifting the accelerator foot, then shifting before depressing the accelerator again – doesn't sound hard but some drivers have difficulty mastering the technique.

Will it fit in the garage?

Saloons

Length	(1967-1975)	4874mm (191.9in)
Width	(1966-1967)	1790mm (70.5in)
Width	(1968-1975)	1803mm (71.0in)

Breaks

Length	(1966-1967)	4990mm (196.5in)
Length	(1968-1975)	5026mm (197.9in)
Width	(1968-1975)	1803mm (71.0in)

Interior space

There are seatbelts for four people but the D-model could quite comfortably carry a fifth adult in the back. The Breaks have either two small jump seats in the back or a third-row seat in the Break Familiale. Legroom and headroom are plentiful with large, wide-opening doors for easy entry and exit.

The suspension level in its lowest position.

The inner headlamps turn with the steering.

Luggage capacity

The Saloon's 16.6ft³ boot (trunk) is big enough to accommodate almost everyone's luggage requirements. The Break's carrying capability is legendary – the fold-flat rear seat, cavernous loading area, clam-like opening rear hatch, and the car's ability to adjust to numerous loading heights made it an ideal commercial vehicle during its heyday.

Running costs

Oil changes should be done every 3000 miles, or at least once a year if used conservatively. The 4-cylinder engine's basic design originated with the 1934 Citroën 11CV and was also used in many Citroën commercial vehicles until the 1980s – and for good reason: the engine is sturdy and reliable – in some cases managing 250,000 miles or more before requiring an overhaul. The hydraulics will require regular maintenance – including frequent fluid changes (every 2 years on the older LHS2 models) and replacement, every 6-7 years, of the nitrogen-filled accumulators and spheres.

The ID19 and D Special with the single-barrel Solex carburettor will achieve decent mileage in the mid-to-high twenties range, whereas DS models – with the thirstier Weber – will manage around 20mpg. The fuel-injected DS23 is even thirstier – barely managing 18mpg.

Usability

Performance is anaemic by modern standards – especially on the ID19 and D Special. The 5-speed-equipped DS23 EFi performance is more respectable – with a 0-60mph time of around 10 seconds. Although there are still many owners who use their D-model as the primary vehicle, most current owners consider it a fun second car or hobby car rather than a daily driver.

Parts availability

Most items are readily available – even more so now than 10 years ago. There are several aftermarket manufacturers who have copied and remanufactured almost every maintenance and trim item on the car – even most of the body panels have been remanufactured in fibreglass.

Parts costs
Most maintenance parts are very reasonable – transmission gear and bearing costs are expensive, as are some of the stainless steel trim items.

Insurance
Insurance can be quite reasonable, especially if the vehicle is used as a hobby car with a classic/collector insurance policy.

Investment potential
Excellent – the Citroën D-model has been appreciating steadily in value during the last 5 years – owners can probably even recoup the cost of a rust-free D-model purchase and a home restoration at the time of resale – unlikely with most other classics.

Foibles
Waiting for the car to rise after startup can irritate some impatient drivers. A hydraulic leak will disable the suspension, brakes, steering, and, on the Citromatic-equipped cars, even the gear change.

Plus points
Unmatched comfort and roadability coupled with a unique look and design.

Minus points
Wind noise through unframed door windows. Mediocre gas mileage. Hydraulic layout can be daunting for an inexperienced mechanic. A badly maintained hydraulic system could easily turn your car into a money pit. Rust could be hidden under carpets and rust-proofing. Some repairs, such as timing chain, clutch and front brake discs, are very time-consuming and thus expensive to do. Beware of hidden rust in floorboards, chassis sidemembers and boot floor.

The D-model's unique headlamp system making a right turn.

Alternatives
None that could directly compare to the Citroën D – possible considerations: the Peugeot 504, Alfa Romeo Giulia, Lancia Fulvia or Rover 2000TC – some buyers might consider the 1976-1990 Citroën CX: the car that replaced the D-series.

2 Cost considerations
– affordable, or a money pit?

This straight rust-free USA-market car, needing paint, would probably be an affordable and smart purchase.

This D, created for a museum, details the complexity of the hydraulics and front-wheel-drive mechanicals.

Unless you are an experienced mechanic or insist on having a car finished to your exact tastes, buying a cheap fixer-upper D-model is rarely a smart move. Restoring a DS or ID, especially a car with hydraulic or rust issues, can quickly empty anyone's bank account. Restoring a DS can cost ●x20,000 or more, whereas an excellent rust-free car can be bought for around half that amount.

Having said that, a lot of owners enjoy the restoration process and prefer the option of finishing the car to their own paint, upholstery and trim specification. But coupled with the ultimate higher cost, the restoration process also means it might be several years before you will be driving and enjoying your car.

The final, and in my eyes, riskiest, route to an excellent D-model is to buy a below-average condition but drivable car that will be restored on weekends and as finances allow. The problem with this route is that these 'rolling restorations' quickly become immobile full restorations

due to the complexity of the car's hydraulics and mechanics. The makeup of the car is not such that one can keep it running and drivable while spending a bit on it every other week – optimistic owners quickly become discouraged and the cars have a habit of seeing high ownership turnover until finding a more realistic and determined buyer.

Servicing

Many of the replacement parts (especially the hydraulics) could be worn by time rather than mileage.

Service intervals

Basic oil change: Every 3000 miles or 3 months
Minor tuneup: Every 6000 miles or 12 months
Major tuneup: Every 12,000 miles
Valve adjustment: Every 15,000 miles
Hydraulic flush: Every 2 years (especially recommended on LHS2 models)

Parts costs

(with approximate hours needed to install the part)

Front brake pads: x75 (1.2 hours)
Rear brake shoes: x40 (3.0 hours)
Emergency brake pads: x40 (5.0 hours)
Front brake discs: x125 (7.0 hours)
Hydraulic pump: x200 (2-4 hours depending on model)
Front suspension spheres: x80 (0.5 hours)
Rear suspension spheres: x80 (1.0 hours)
Head gasket: x37.5 (5-8 hours depending on model)
Timing chain kit: x90 (12-16 hours depending on model – engine needs to be removed)
Clutch set: x200 (10-14 hours depending on model)
Hydraulic steering rack: x450 (5 hours)
Mechanical fuel pump: x37.5 (1.0 hours)
Exhaust system: x225 (1.5 hours)
Radiator: x225 (2.0 hours)
Water pump (non-AC): x80 (4-6 hours depending on model)
Alternator: x150 (1½ hours)
Starter: x200 (1½-3 hours depending on model)
Carburettor: x175 (2 hours)

This ID19 engine bay is simple with lots of access room and relatively little complexity.

Bodywork

(replacement time listed – does not include time needed to exchange trim or paint)

Bonnet (hood) (used): x300 (2.0 hours)
Door (used): x200 (1.0 hours)
Windscreen: x250 (2.0 hours)
Door glass (used): x40 (2.0 hours)
Rear wing (used): x150 (0.3 hours)
Front wing (used): x225 (1.0 hours)
Front bumper (used): x250 (3.0 hours)
Rear bumper (used): x200 (1.0 hours)

This later Citromatic engine bay is more complex with tighter work space.

Centreline trim set: x225 (6.0 hours)
Front headlight glass: x80 (2.5 hours)
Repaint (average): x2500

Interior
Leather upholstery installed: x1600
Cloth upholstery installed: x1100
Headliner: x150
Carpet installed: x300
Door panels installed: x700

Parts that are hard to find: There is a tremendous aftermarket parts source for the 1966 to 1975 D-model and most parts are readily available. A few items that you might have a hard time finding are switches, bonnets, rust-free replacement body panels and some of the fuel-injection components and stainless steel bumper pieces.

Parts that are expensive: Most parts are affordable by Classic car standards although a bonnet or steering rack replacement could set you back in excess of x500 – especially when the labour costs are factored in.

This intimidating EFi engine bay is a mass of hoses, pipes and wires. You are likely to need a specialist for the majority of maintenance work.

Only this single rear bolt has to be unscrewed to remove the rear wing.

Summary
Virtually nothing compares to the ride and comfort of the Citroën D-model. Many a back-seat passenger has compared the car's ride to sitting on an overstuffed cushy couch. Its innovative hydraulic suspension, dramatic aerodynamic design, and glass-encased turning headlights (from September 1967 onward) make the D-model a head-turner and a unique and avant-garde ownership statement. A common refrain about the Citroën D-model is that it is 'ugly to behold – but once a passenger and you are sold.'

Good points
Incomparable ride comfort
Plenty of head and legroom
Great driver visibility
Front-wheel-drive roadholding
Decent performance on DS23 and fuel-injected models
Unique design
Excellent braking system
Ease of changing a tire with adjustable suspension

This late-sixties curved dash shows the radio placement and an early AC installation.

Most body panels can be removed easily within minutes
Most maintenance work can be done by owner
Simple and reliable engine
Accident-safe because of front and rear crumple zones
Stainless steel bumpers and trim
Large boot
Great parts availability
Can be a daily driver with correct maintenance

Bad points
Cost of restoration
Some of the work can only be done by a Citroën specialist
Lack of factory rust-proofing can make it susceptible to frame corrosion
Frameless windows allow excessive air noise
Bolted-down roof can allow leaks into the passenger compartment
Fuel consumption is mediocre on DS21 and DS23 versions
The fuel-injection system increases time taken on simple maintenance tasks
Some fuel-injection parts are difficult to source
Hydraulic system can be daunting to inexperienced mechanics
Poorly maintained hydraulic system can be a maintenance nightmare
Front inboard brakes can be expensive to repair
Lots of good-looking but badly maintained cars on the market
Good luck finding a radio that fits in a dashboard from 1970 on
Radio controls are hard to reach for the driver in 1966-1969 cars
Hard to find cars with sunroof and AC options

The 4 small vents in this bumper blade supplies airflow to the left valance-mounted AC condensor.

This chapter will give you an idea, expressed as a percentage, of the value of individual models in good condition. For example, a good 1970s DS21 Pallas currently sells for about ⬤x6000 at the time of writing, whereas a good mid-1960s ID19 might fetch only ⬤x2500. Excellent or restored cars will realise even more – a rusty basket case might be barely worth the cost of towing it.

It's unlikely you will find a cheap Cabriolet but they are worth the search.

This 1966 DS21 has been tarted up and is equipped with valance-mounted driving lights, hood handle and fender-mounted driving lights.

Cabriolets

The Chapron convertibles (factory and Carrossier versions) and Coupés can't really be included in this formula. The convertibles are currently commanding stratospheric prices – typically 3 to 5 times as much as similar-condition Sedans. Less than 1400 of these factory convertibles were constructed in a 12-year period and, when they do become available for sale, are typically heavily advertised to fetch the best possible price.

Do be aware of Chapron fakes – there have been many attempts in the last

This beautiful 1966 Break has the optional teardrop driving lights.

30 years to copy Chapron's handiwork. Some of these are obvious copies – fibreglass rear bodies with smaller non-Chapron doors and rear bumpers – but some are harder to spot. There have

also been some instances of owners buying rusted-out Chapron shells for their paperwork and serial number tags, and using another D Sedan or Wagon to then build an 'original' Chapron. These 'resurrected' Chaprons have more value than the copies but less than a totally original car.

Values

The following are approximate values – the most sought-after and priciest models listed at 100% and the rest shown as a percentage of that value. These prices are a reflection of good condition, original cars. ID models that have been modified to DS mechanicals and/or trim, and DS Citromatic versions that have been changed to 4-speed or 5-speed manual trim should only be valued as the original car. Some buyers will pay extra for such modified cars but consider that these modifications might affect future value. I have tried to keep the list manageable and have not differentiated between Pallas and non-Pallas models, or included added values for a leather interior or AC. As a rough rule of thumb, a Pallas version is worth about 20% more than a non-Pallas version, and a leather or factory-installed AC (only after 1972 with vented front bumpers) will add another 5%. I also haven't included the Prestige model, a Chapron-built limousine version of the DS, which had a partition separating front and rear passengers. The Prestige was offered by Citroën from 1958 to 1974 but built in relatively small numbers – it is probably worth around 30% more than the non-Prestige version.

Although a bit of a hybrid (it has both USA and European trim), this 1972 DS21 is very attractive and well presented.

This attractive 1975 DS23 EFi has the bumper-mounted AC condensers.

DS & ID Sedan models

1973-1975 DS23 Sedan EFi 5-speed. 100%
1973-1975 DS23 Sedan carburated 5-speed. 95%
1973-1975 DS23 Sedan EFi Citromatic 90%
1973-1975 DS23 Sedan carburated Citromatic 85%
1970-1972 DS21 Sedan EFi manual trans 85%
1970-1972 DS21 Sedan EFi Citromatic 80%
1970-1972 DS21 Sedan carburated manual trans 75%
1970-1972 DS21 Sedan carburated Citromatic 70%
1973-1975 D Super 5 . . . . 65%
1970-1975 DS20 . . . . 60%
1970-1975 D Super 55%
1970-1975 D Special 50%
1967-1969 DS21 (LHM hydraulics). 60%
1966 DS21 (LHS2 hydraulics). 50%
1967-1969 DS19 (LHM hydraulics). 45%
1966 DS19 (LHS2 hydraulics). 40%
1967-1969 ID19 (LHM hydraulics) 40%
1966 ID19 (LHS2 hydraulics) 35%

It must be noted that USA models, which have been imported back to the continent in large numbers, only received the mineral-based LHM hydraulics in mid-1969 – therefore, USA models with earlier LHS2 hydraulics should be similarly priced to the 1966 version in the list above.

The simple interior of a
Citroën ID19.

The Breaks or Familiale versions of the D-model, although produced in smaller numbers and harder to find in better-than-average condition, are not as highly prized or sought-after as the Sedan versions. Therefore, using the list above, value the Break and Familiale at 90% of its Sedan version.

The DS Pallas has a much higher trim
level than an ID or DS.

The Pallas' well-appointed interior is the
height of comfort and style.

5 Before you view
– be well informed

To avoid the frustration of a car not meeting your expectations, be sure to ask specific questions when you call before viewing. Excitement about buying a D-model can mean even obvious things slip your mind, and it's harder for sellers to answer very specific questions dishonestly. Try to assess the attitude and demeanour of the seller, and decide how comfortable you are buying a used car from him or her.

Where is the car?
Work out the cost of travelling to view a car. For a rare model, such as a Chapron or a cabriolet, it may be worth travelling but if your target purchase is a common D-model, decide how far you are prepared to go. You might first want to educate yourself on locally advertised cars if any are available.

Dealer or private sale?
Is the seller the owner of the car or a dealer? Private owners are more likely to have a detailed history of the car and be more likely to answer detailed questions. Dealers, if they are not Citroën-specific, may know less about the car. Some

This small round plaque at the top right corner of the firewall lists the original paint code (code starts with AC).

Citroën-specific dealers might be worth approaching if they have numerous models available or the ability to put you on a waiting list for a specified year, model or trim level.

Cost of collection and delivery?
Dealers may deliver, but, unless arranged as part of the sale, it probably won't be cheap. Private owners may meet you halfway, especially if the car is roadworthy, but be sure to view the car at the seller's address beforehand to verify its condition and validate paperwork and ownership.

Viewing – when and where?
It's always preferable to view the car at the seller's home or business. A private seller's name and address should be on the title documents unless there's a good reason why not. Try to view the car in daylight and dry weather when it will be easier to spot bodywork flaws and rust.

Reason for sale?
Genuine sellers will explain why they are selling and their length of ownership. They may also know something about previous owners.

Conversions and specials
Many Pallas models started life as a plain DS21, many leather outfitted cars were originally cloth, many DS21 models are converted ID19s – if it matters to you that the car is factory original then ask the seller if he is aware of any conversions. Only about 21,500 right-hand-drive D-models were sold in the UK market over a 19-year period so it is more likely that you will find a left-hand-drive version – if it is critical for you that the car is right-hand-drive then keep looking until you find one as no one is currently converting them.

A significant number of cars have been imported from the USA – cars that might be rust-free (if purchased from California or Arizona) but might originally have been outfitted with different headlights, body trim, or even smog systems. The conversion of USA cars to European specification doesn't necessarily diminish the value of the car unless conversion work was poorly done.

The serial number on the plate should match the number punched into the firewall ledge.

Condition? (body/chassis/interior/mechanics)
Try to get an idea of the car's condition in terms as specific as possible – if the seller reveals some flaws in the car that you are unwilling to put up with or repair, then it will save you the cost of further investigation. Use the checklist in the later chapters as a guide.

All original specification?
An unchanged original car will be of higher value than a converted car. However, some conversions could actually add to the value of the car – especially if your plan for your car is to drive it rather than win a trophy at a concours. It is not uncommon to find a 5-speed transmission on a car that left the factory with a 4-speed. A well-installed late version of the air conditioning is highly prized and sought-after by many buyers.

6 Inspection equipment
– these items will really help

This book
This book covers the major defects that you are likely to find on a Citroën D-model. Keep this book handy while doing a step-by-step inspection – if the car has any of the faults outlined in it then you are likely to find them.

Magnet and rag
Using a rag as a buffer between the magnet and bodywork (to avoid scratching the paint), run the magnet along the car's bodywork. If there are thick layers of body filler then the magnet won't stick – remember that the magnet will not work on the aluminium bonnet and fibreglass roof.

Overalls
Wearing overalls will allow you to crawl under and around the D-model to inspect for any rust or leaks. A word of warning: if the D's hydraulic suspension has an internal pressure leak then it could quickly and suddenly drop from its highest to lowest level – it is advised that you do not crawl under the car unless you have a support stand in place to prevent such a drop.

Rubber garden glove
A rubber glove will come in handy with the engine balance test – you will be removing a spark plug wire while the car is running and the glove will prevent a nasty shock.

Flashlight
Use a flashlight to inspect the side of the engine for leaks and the bottom of the chassis for rust.

Screwdriver
With the approval of the car's owner, use a screwdriver to poke the undercoating for rust along the edge and back of the chassis.

Watch
A watch is needed to record recycling time of the hydraulics under different conditions.

Camera
Bring along a camera to record areas of concern – you could then, at a later date, show your photos to a mechanic to get a more informed opinion.

Pen and paper
Detailed notes for yourself or to get mechanical estimates are always a good idea – especially if you are inspecting more than one car before you decide on your purchase.

7 Fifteen minute evaluation
– walk away or stay?

Do a cursory inspection for leaks.

When looking at a prospective D-model for the first time, it's important to harden your resolve not to buy the first basket case that you set eyes on. Body and paintwork, which most of us are unlikely to tackle, will be the most expensive repairs. Having said that, how much of the mechanical, electrical or trim work are you capable of taking on yourself? That answer should help you decide on the quality of car that you are about to purchase. If you are unable, or unwilling, to take on a significant amount of repair then buy the best car possible and avoid the 'handyman delights'. If you are a more accomplished and mechanical buyer then you might be willing to overlook significant deficiencies to purchase a D at a lower price. Whatever your final D might be – a pristine 1966 ID19 or a ratty but running DS23 EFi – there are some cars that you should walk away from.

There are several important points to initial inspection – the first, and probably most important one, should be the sills (rockers) along the left and right side of the chassis and the floorboards. Look underneath the car along the edge of the chassis and the front floorboard (approximately where the front foot well would be). Are there any rust holes? Has it got dimples in it, or is it a flat sheet of steel? Are there any suspicious welds, rivets or bolts to suggest rust repair? Is there an excessive amount of undercoating that might be covering up rust or rust repairs? Rust along the sills is almost impossible to repair correctly and any evidence that would suggest the presence of rust, or extensive repairs to correct rust, should probably make you walk away immediately.

If the sills pass inspection, lift the carpets and inspect the floorboards. Do the floorboards look solid and rust-free? Do the floorboards look original or might they be replacements? Is there any road hazard or jacking damage on the floor boards? The later deficiencies are probably acceptable to most of us, but carefully inspect for any further evidence of rust or repair to decide if this is a car worth considering.

Lift the front mats to inspect the floorboards.

Open the bonnet and check the front subframe directly behind the bumper and next to the radiator. Look for any wrinkles in the metal suggesting a frontal impact. The

Look along the frame sills for evidence of rust or damage.

subframe is difficult to pull straight because of its softer metal and, although it can be replaced, this needs to be done correctly to ensure the front body panels are properly aligned and spaced. Decide if you want to deal with the hassle or move on to the next possibility.

Open the doors and appraise all the pillars. Rust in the doors can be corrected by repair panels, or even just exchanging for another door, but the pillars can be a little tougher to correct. Check at the bottom of each pillar and the top of the front door pillars where the hood hinges are bolted. If there is rust present in the pillars, gauge its severity to decide whether or not to proceed.

At the back of the car, look from underneath at the boot floor. Does it look sound? If not, how bad is it? Replacement floorboards are available but you don't want to deal with rust that is too close to the chassis beams. Inspect the rear suspension cylinders and condition of the chassis directly next to the suspension cylinder and sphere. If the chassis is rusty in this area then the pressure generated by the suspension as the car lifts and responds to road conditions, could buckle the metal and make the car unusable and virtually unrepairable. Avoid cars with any frame buckles or extensive rust near the rear suspension.

Stand in front of the car and check the upright stance of the front tyres. The D-model does not have an adjustment for camber and caster, so an odd angle to the tyres cannot be corrected by adjustment. An odd stance could be attributed to a bent suspension arm – a rather expensive repair and, unless you are buying the car at a significant discount, reason to walk away and keep searching.

Lift the oil cap and radiator cap – check for oil in the water and water in the oil. Either scenario would entail extensive mechanical repair and, unless you are prepared to undertake those repairs and the car is priced accordingly, would be another reason to keep looking through the classifieds.

The cosmetics of the car, the paint and interior, should meet your personal standards or expectations. Are you looking for a concours car? – then a faded DS21 with bumper dings, a combo vinyl/leather interior and white puffs coming from the exhaust probably doesn't meet your standards. Or, you might be shopping for the perfect restoration project – a ratty car with average mechanicals and little-to-no rust. The perfect car for one buyer might be completely wrong for another. Your initial impression and approval of the quality of the paint, interior and trim got you this far – and if the car passed our above cursory inspection then it might be time to proceed with Chapter 9 – serious evaluation.

Check under the rear for leaks and rust.

8 Key points

– where to look for problems

Key aspects to check on D-models are:

Chassis rust
Unless you are lucky enough to find a D-model from either south Europe or southern USA, then the D-model you are considering will either exhibit some rust or some evidence of attempts to halt or repair rust. Rust repairs, if done professionally, should not deter you from considering the car if the rest of the vehicle is in sound shape. There are a wide variety of aftermarket repair panels available for the D, and rust in most body panels – and even the floorboards – can be repaired without affecting the integrity of the rest of the car. However, substantial rust along the edge of the car's chassis and next to the rear suspension cylinders will probably establish the car as a parts-donor vehicle rather than a daily driver.

DS rocker panels make it difficult to inspect the frame sills for rust or damage.

Hydraulics
Although the D-model's hydraulic system is its most recognized strength, it could also be its greatest weakness. A poorly maintained hydraulic system can have a myriad of problems – some problems not evident until another one is fixed. A hydraulic pump with short recycling times could indicate a variety of problems, including worn suspension cylinders, internal leak in the steering rack, a tired pump, or several other possibilities. Checking for dryness around all of the hydraulic components, lines and hoses does not ensure that the system is in good working order.

Electrical wiring

If you are considering a 1966 to 1969 D-model then carefully inspect the main wiring harness – especially where it enters the firewall and connects to the front fenders. The wiring harness used between 1966 and 1969 had an inferior insulation wrap that would frequently deteriorate to bare wire – an accident waiting to happen. Aftermarket wiring harnesses (identical to the OE Citroën harness, but with better insulation) are now available. Bare wires or poorly repaired wires are an indication that some money will have to be spent on this aspect of the car.

Transmission

Test the integrity of the transmission gears, synchros and bearings while test driving the car. Overhauling a transmission on a D can be even more expensive than an engine rebuild – there are several gears and bearings in the transmission that cost ⬤x150 to ⬤x250, thus, ensuring that the car has a sound transmission could save you thousands.

Engine condition

The design of the D's four-cylinder engine was 21 years old when the DS19 was first introduced in 1955. Although the engine was updated in 1966, it retained its 4-cylinder design layout and was the only engine, in several variations, offered throughout the D-model's entire production history – and with good reason. The engine is very robust and a well-maintained engine can survive for 250,000 miles or more before needing a rebuild. Having said that, there are plenty of poorly maintained D engines and recognizing that an engine is nearing the end of its productive life could stop you from buying the car or, at the very least, call for a much lower purchase price.

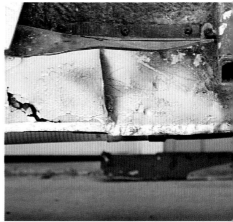

This rust was hidden behind a rocker panel and was difficult to spot.

www.velocebooks.com / www.veloce.co.uk
All current books • New book news • Special offers • Gift vouchers

9 Serious evaluation
– 60 minutes for years of enjoyment

Exterior
Paintwork   Ex [4]   Gd [3]   Av [2]   Po [1]

Inspect the car's paintwork and decide if it meets your standards. Repainting a car can be very expensive, especially if done correctly. It takes a lot of time to remove door handles, body rubbers and body trim and, if you are planning a colour change, this would necessitate removing the interior trim and door panels, too. If the car has recently been repainted check the paint for gloss and depth – a foggy orange peel look is probably a good indication that it was done on the cheap. Your magnet and rag will come in handy here – run them along the body, especially along the bottom of the doors, front and rear fenders and below the headlights, to check for body filler. If you are viewing the car in good sunlight, walk around it to check for waves in the body and disappearing body lines – if the car has had budget body work the sharp body lines (running at about 8 inches from the bottom of the doors and wings) will be flattened or rounded off. Poorly repaired dents will have been fixed by slapping on vast amounts of filler, rather than having been pulled and hammered out, resulting in non-adherence of your magnet.

Body panels
Overall structure   Ex [4]   Gd [3]   Av [2]   Po [1]

Go to one rear corner, kneel down and look along the body lines to ensure that they are consistent. Do the same on the opposite side. If one side's body lines are drastically different than the opposite side, suspect a poorly repaired accident or inferior body work.

Body gaps   Ex [4]   Gd [3]   Av [2]   Po [1]

Walk around the car and check the wing and door gaps – they should all be around ⅜in and consistent from front to rear of the car. Are there excessive and inconsistent gaps on one side of the car? – if so, it is likely that the suspect side suffered an accident and was poorly repaired.

The body gaps are uneven on this car but can probably be adjusted.

Exterior trim   Ex [4]   Gd [3]   Av [2]   Po [1]

The ID19 and D Special have very little trim, but DS cars, especially the Pallas models, have an inordinate amount of mouldings running along the body. Check to see if the car has a complete set of mouldings; more importantly, check around them for rust bubbles – the mouldings are stainless steel but trap mud and water, so are common areas to rust.

This side shot of the DS shows a myriad of mouldings on the car.

Look for rust underneath the front headlights.

Below headlights
Ex 4 Gd 3 Av 2 Po 1

Inspect the front wings under the headlights and around the front indicator assemblies. The double layers of metal in this area, notorious for rust, will be expensive to repair.

Front valance
Ex 4 Gd 3 Av 2 Po 1

Inspect the front valance closely – this commonly has rust holes at its lowest points but also might have a large amount of filler to mask previous parking mishaps. Fortunately, affordable fibreglass valances are available to replace panels that might be excessively damaged or rusted.

Rust at the leading edge of this D's front wheel well was probably the result of trapped mud.

Front wings
Ex 4 Gd 3 Av 2 Po 1

Check the lower part of the front wings behind the wheel – if no rust is evident then reach in under the wing to feel for any rust holes. Several mud flaps are located at the rear of the front wings that could trap mud and cause rust.

Engine bay
Ex 4 Gd 3 Av 2 Po 1

Inspect the front subframe in the engine bay. The front subframe is softer than the rest of the chassis to allow it to collapse during a frontal accident and absorb the impact. Unfortunately, smaller accidents might have caused wrinkles and bends in the subframe that may have been left untreated – check with a flashlight at each side of the radiator and behind the front bumper.

Bottom of doors
Ex 4 Gd 3 Av 2 Po 1

Although showing its age, this door bottom is entirely rust- and crack-free.

Check for straightness along the bottom of the doors – there shouldn't be a noticeable curve. Check for rust bubbles, especially at the front lower corners of the front doors. Open the doors and check for rust, cracks and repairs at the lower back of all four doors.

Rust at the bottom front corner of a D's left front door.

Top of front doors
Ex 4 Gd 3 Av 2 Po 1

Check for cracks at the outside mirror mounts and the top front inside corner of the doors. The front doors are large and heavy and, after 35+ years of slamming shut, are apt to have cracks at these front stress points. Small cracks are weldable but larger cracks can be difficult to correct to your cosmetic satisfaction.

Rear wings
Ex 4 Gd 3 Av 2 Po 1

Open the rear doors and check the inner walls of the rear wings where they mount on their front mounting pins – this is the most likely area of rust.

Rust is common along the bottom edge of the boot lid.

This is a healthy, rust- and damage-free rear wing pillar.

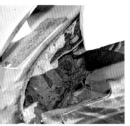

This close-up shows rust next to the bonnet hinge – difficult to repair.

Boot lid

Citroën glued a large sponge-type seal to the inside of the D-model's boot lid to prevent water from entering the boot area. Unfortunately, the seal's protective coating chips off with age and, because of its sponge-like material, soaks up water as it rusts the boot lid from the inside out. The worst rust will be along the bottom edge of the lid. Also check for stress cracks about halfway down each side – the lid's flimsy framework, especially if aggravated by the added weight of the water-soaked seal, has a tendency to collapse.

Door pillars

Inspect the bottom of the four door pillars and the rear wing pillars for rust, as they can be trapping points for water and mud. Also check for poorly or unrepaired damage on each pillar – a budget repair on a side impact might have entailed repairing or replacing the outer body panels but structural pillars might have been ignored.

Bonnet

The bonnet is typically not a concern on most cars, but the aluminium bonnet used on the D-model can be plagued by both corrosion and stress cracks. Check the front inside edge of the bonnet for cracks and corrosion – and the side edges of the bonnet for cracks. If there is evidence that the bonnet has flipped (common if not latched correctly) it will be difficult to repair and you will probably have to source a replacement (new ones are no longer available and good used ones are expensive).

The aluminium bonnet frequently develops cracks along the edges.

Also inspect the top of the A-pillar where the bonnet hinges are bolted to the car. Leaves, mud and water will collect around the hinges and rot away the mounting area – anything beyond minor rust will require reconstruction of the top of the A-pillar.

Roof

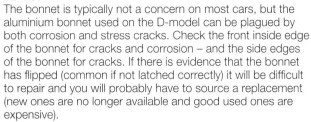

The roof is another area of the D-model not usually of concern for most conventional cars. The D-model, however, has a bolted-down fibreglass roof with a U-shaped seal along the roof's metal outer edge. There are two related problem areas on the roof – the first is the seal which tends to harden and

The aluminium corrosion on this bonnet was probably aggravated by inferior bodywork.

This roof seal is cracked and badly deteriorated – close examination will be needed to ensure a seal replacement is possible for the roof's metal edge.

This Estate (Wagon) roof shows an attempt to repair a leaking roof seal – the Estate roof will suffer from worse rust than the sedan as it is steel instead of fibreglass.

crack with age – this leads to water leaks in the passenger compartment and staining of the headliner. A leaking seal can also contribute to the other problem – rust on the metal edge of the fibreglass roof. This edge, which is bonded to the fibreglass, will eventually rust to the point that it separates from the fibreglass; without this edge there is no longer any means to keep the roof bolted on the car. Carefully inspect the roof seal – check for any rust bubbles creeping up from beneath the seal – if warranted, lift the rubber seal with a small screwdriver to inspect the metal edge.

Windscreen frame

Ex [4] Gd [3] Av [2] Po [1]

The D-model's windscreen sits in a rubber seal that is pressed up and into the windscreen frame. This makes it relatively easy to exchange the windscreen as only a large bracket, at the bottom of the windscreen, needs to be unbolted. However, because the windscreen is not glued in, the encasing rubber can be a trap for water – especially along the top of the windscreen/front of the roof. Lift the rubber away from the windscreen frame to check for rust damage – excessive rust damage could mean replacing rather than repairing the upper frame rail. Be wary of cars that have a liberal amount of sealant around the windscreen frame and rubber.

Rear bumper

Ex [4] Gd [3] Av [2] Po [1]

The rear bumper blades and uprights are stainless – they can be straightened and polished if necessary. Grab the bumper and attempt to move it up and down – if there is any movement at all the bumper mounts at the far sides of the rear boot wall will likely have rot issues. At this point you might want to remove the rear wings (one bolt at the end of the wings) to inspect a little more closely.

Rear boot wall

Ex [4] Gd [3] Av [2] Po [1]

Inspect the top of the rear boot wall – especially in the corners. A bad boot lid seal and wet climate will result in rust along this ledge. Replacement boot walls are available if rust is excessive.

Boot floor & sidewalls

Ex [4] Gd [3] Av [2] Po [1]

Lift the boot floor mat and inspect the boot floor – it is also vulnerable to rust. Fortunately, replacement boot floors are available. Also look along the bottom of the boot walls – lift the boot matting again if necessary. The boot floor and walls are probably the most common areas for rust on the D – mostly because so many cars have bad boot lid seals. Even if rust is not found, make sure to check for any wrinkles in the walls and floor which would indicate an unrepaired rear accident.

Rear 'tow' hooks

Ex [4] Gd [3] Av [2] Po [1]

Inspect the 'tow' hooks by looking under the rear bumper at the rear ledge of the

This D's 'tow' hook was yanked loose when it was used as a tie-down.

Although the rest of this car is rust-free, a bad boot seal rotted out the back boot ledge.

boot sill. Even though they are referred to as 'tow' hooks, these hooks are really little more than strong points for jacking up the rear of the car. If these hooks were used to tie down the car during transportation then chances are there will either be holes where the hooks used to be, or they are partially ripped loose from the boot sill. If you do need to tie down the car for towing strap down either the rear wheels (the rear wings can be easily removed for access), or the rear suspension arms (being careful not to pinch any hydraulic lines).

An untouched 'tow' hook under the rear bumper.

Frame sills

☒4 ☒3 ☒2 ☒1

Rust attacked this right rear door sill rubber retaining strip.

The frame sills on the ID and Break can be easily inspected – unfortunately, the DS and Pallas frame sills are covered with large rocker panels and cannot be inspected without removal of these panels. The seller of the car will probably not allow you to remove the panels, so you might have to suffice with inspecting the small areas of the sills that are visible through the two rocker panel access holes and the small uncovered areas at the front of the rocker panels. These access holes and uncovered areas are meant as jacking points but are large enough to allow some poking with a screwdriver and inspection with a flashlight.

Floors

☒4 ☒3 ☒2 ☒1

Lift the front and rear floor mats to check for rust – especially where the frame sills join the floorboards. The foam backing on the D-model's floor mats are apt to retain water so the boards could rust from the inside out. Sill and floorboard repair panels are available but be prepared to pay for dozens of hours to correctly install those panels.

Lights

☒4 ☒3 ☒2 ☒1

The post-1967 D-model has a glass-covered quad headlight setup. On most of these cars, the centre high beams swivel with the direction of the steering and level with changes in the suspension height. Used parts are readily available to repair any headlight problems, but inspect the headlight silvering and functionality of the swivelling and levelling as you will probably have to hire a specialist for any repairs.

Inspect the beams for good silvering. Used parts can be readily sourced for any 'turning' issues.

Body seals

☒4 ☒3 ☒2 ☒1

Virtually any body seal is available from a Citroën D specialist but your inspection should not necessarily be for seal replacement but rather other accompanying problems. A bad roof, door, boot or body seal will allow water into these areas and result in rust. Inspect for cracked, worn or hard seals – following up with a more in-depth inspection of the body area around the suspect seal.

This view towards the interior rear of a Estate shows heavy rust in the typical problem areas.

Estate problems

Ex	Gd	Av	Po
4	3	2	1

From the rear doors forward, the D Estate (also known as a Break, Wagon, Safari or Familiale) is identical to the Sedan version of the D. There are only minor mechanical differences in the rear suspension and brakes of the Estate – none that would cause different issues or problems. There are, however, several cosmetic differences on the rear of the Estate that have an increased potential for rust. The upper area of the Estate's inner wheel well (where it joins the frame of the rear quarter window) will

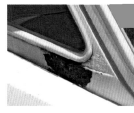

The rust around this Estate's left rear quarter window will be difficult and expensive to fix.

collect mud and dirt, thereby trapping moisture and rotting the metal – shine your flashlight inside the top of the wheel well – remove the rear fender if a closer inspection is warranted.

The rear quarter window rubbers are also traps for moisture – inspect the lower portion of the window frames (inside as well as outside) for rust bubbling. Excessive rust in this area will be difficult to repair.

Inspect the larger upper tailgate around the window rubber – rust on the tailgate is more commonly found on the inside, so carefully inspect around the lower inner section of the window rubber.

Another 'typical' Estate rust area is at the lower inside corners of the rear hatch.

Wheels and tyres

Ex	Gd	Av	Po
4	3	2	1

The D has steel disc wheels with stainless steel hubcaps (a very low quality stainless steel on the ID, D Special and D Super versions) – inspect for damage along the outer edge of the wheel and corrosion along wheel seams. Used replacement wheels are widely available so inferior items are not a deal-breaker. Also inspect the tyres – the original Michelin XAS tyres are very expensive, and cheaper aftermarket options are usually not an exact match in size (larger and smaller sized tyres can affect the car's steering, handling and speedometer reading).

Exhaust

Ex	Gd	Av	Po
4	3	2	1

Check the exhaust manifold bolted between the engine and the down pipe – there should be no hissing or blowing noises at the fittings, which would indicate either a blown gasket or, worse still, a broken manifold stud. Replacing a broken stud in the cylinder head could be time-consuming – especially if the broken stud is towards the back of the engine where there is little room for manoeuvring a stud extractor.

This D-model should have dual exhaust pipes, thus, this single pipe should be a clue that the car has a non-original system – probably welded together.

The exhaust down pipe connects to a flexible pipe which connects into a traverse-mounted muffler, followed by dual outlet pipes. The outlet pipes could also be connected into a rear silencer. Inspect the exhaust system for age, rust and holes. Also check to ensure that all components are clamped together – a common exhaust quick fix is to weld the connections, which repairs any leaks but makes it difficult to replace an individual component.

Removing the rear fenders (easily done) will allow you to closely inspect the rear wheel well area.

Glass

Ex   Gd   Av   Po
[4]   [3]   [2]   [1]

The windscreen is not glued in and can easily be exchanged – check for cracks, deep scratches and excessive pitting. Check the guides on the door glass – this is done by winding the door window to the half position, grasping the top of the glass and attempting to move the window in and out. There should be very little movement – worn guides will not only cause rattles but also an ineffective window seal against the door frame, thereby allowing entry of water and wind.

Interior
Seats

Ex   Gd   Av   Po
[4]   [3]   [2]   [1]

The D-model's seats have been likened to sofas and are considered to be some of the most comfortable ever installed in an automobile. Inspect the quality of the upholstery – is it still the original material, a quality and correct update, or a botched and amateurish replacement? The pre-1969 seats used coil springs, and a flattened appearance to the seat probably indicates that the springs are tired and worn. From 1969 onward, seats used foam innards that held up better to age and use. Adjust the angle of the front seat (a lever on the door-side of the front seats of pre-1969 cars and a round dial for the later cars) to check their function as they sometimes seize from non-use. Slide the seat forward and back (lever in front of seat) as the seat slides might also be stuck. Also, if the car is equipped with them, check the front seat height adjustments (optional on the pre-1971 DS and standard on the later DS) for functionality. Finally, on both front seats, rock back and forth against the seat back to check that the seats are probably secured, as the front securing nuts sometimes tear loose from the seat base.

Door panels

Ex   Gd   Av   Po
[4]   [3]   [2]   [1]

The door panels frequently warp or sag – sometimes to the point that extra screws are required to keep them attached to the doors. Badly warped panels are an indication that water is getting to the panels' backing boards – probably due to cracked window seals at the outside top of the doors.

Headliner

Ex   Gd   Av   Po
[4]   [3]   [2]   [1]

The headliner is either a white vinyl (on earlier ID models) or a light-grey cloth (on most of the later cars). Check for water stains, especially at the front corners, as

The only thing holding the door panel onto this door is the window winder – a leaking outer window seal caused the panel to warp.

Over-tensioning the securing screws of the gauge panel results in these broken corners.

this indicates a bad roof seal and would require the roof to be removed for the seal's replacement.

Carpets

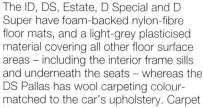

Ex	Gd	Av	Po
4	3	2	1

The ID, DS, Estate, D Special and D Super have foam-backed nylon-fibre floor mats, and a light-grey plasticised material covering all other floor surface areas – including the interior frame sills and underneath the seats – whereas the DS Pallas has wool carpeting colour-matched to the car's upholstery. Carpet kits are now available, so botched carpeting jobs can be easily remedied, albeit at some cost.

Interior door handles

Ex	Gd	Av	Po
4	3	2	1

The handles are plastic, aluminium or chrome-plated pot metal. Although the more upmarket D-models are equipped with the chrome handles, these can actually be the most unsightly. The chrome is likely to chip leaving the potential for very ugly handles in an otherwise good-condition interior. Fortunately, aftermarket handles, although costly, are available through Citroën specialists.

Dashboard and gauges

Ex	Gd	Av	Po
4	3	2	1

Inspect the condition of the dashboard and gauges. The pre-1970 dashboard top is more vulnerable to sun damage and cracking than the later round-dial dashboard (used on all 1970-on cars). However, the later dashboard uses a plastic gauge panel that houses the three round dials and frequently suffers from broken corners. The later dash also isn't very friendly to replacement radios – the factory location is an undersized spot above the ashtray that cannot accept aftermarket radios without having to cut into the dashboard structure. Owners unhappy with the limited space above the ashtray may relocate the radio to the passenger side of the dash below the glovebox. Again, this relocation necessitates more cutting into the dashboard and makes the radio controls difficult for the driver to reach.

Steering wheel

Ex	Gd	Av	Po
4	3	2	1

All versions of the D-model used a single-spoke steering set at the 7o'clock rest position. Prior to 1972, all models had a grey or black spoke wheel with a thin plastic wrap, whereas 1972 and later DS models had a plastic-coated 'safety'

Check the headliner for stains – this one is okay.

This post-1970 dashboard shows a botched attempt at installing a radio.

steering wheel (still with a single spoke). Post-1972 D Special and D super models also received the 'safety' wheel if they were equipped with hydraulically-assisted steering. If the car is equipped with the 'safety' wheel check it for loose covering, as well as overall condition – the steering wheel and column are a single unit; thus, changing the wheel takes a little more time than would be required on a non-D.

Cooling system

Ex   Gd   Av   Po

4️⃣   3️⃣   2️⃣   1️⃣

There are two possible cooling systems on the D. The first, common to the ID and pre-1970 DS cars, uses a down-flow radiator with the pressure cap directly on the radiator. The second system, introduced with the arrival of the DS21 EFi, uses a cross-flow radiator with a secondary temperature-activated electrical fan and the pressure cap on a separate overflow tank. Both are low-pressure systems with belt-driven water pumps and plastic mechanical cooling fans. Cooling air comes from underneath the front bumper, directed to the radiators through an aluminium duct coupled to an upper fabric shroud.

Check for any leak evidence along the top header of the radiator and the body of the water pump – the drain tube on the water pump will drip if the pump has a bad seal.

Check the water pump bearings by grasping the pump's pulley (with the engine turned off) and shaking it to determine any bearing play.

Inspect and feel the condition of the hoses. Are there cracks around the securing clamps? Do the hoses feel hard and brittle or soft and spongy? The hoses should feel stiff but still squeezable – a hard and ungiving hose is likely to crack and a soft spongy hose could be an indication of oil contamination in the cooling system.

Allow the car to idle for at least 20 minutes to gauge the system's cooling ability – overheating might be remedied by replacing a clogged radiator, stuck thermostat, worn water pump (the pump's aluminium impeller could be corroded), broken cooling fan, or possibly even something as simple as exchanging a faulty radiator cap or resetting engine timing. However, overheating can also be caused by internal engine problems and could lead to further complications such as a cracked engine block, blown head gasket or warped cylinder head. Further investigation, by a specialist, might be necessary to determine the cause of the overheating.

Hydraulics
General

Ex   Gd   Av   Po

4️⃣   3️⃣   2️⃣   1️⃣

Inspect the fluid colour through the reservoir's clear side tube. If the car is an earlier LHS2 model the fluid should be almost clear with a slight reddish tinge. The fluid will darken in colour as it ages and will turn foggy or milky with water contamination. The later LHM fluid (as used in cars from 1967 onward in Europe and mid-1969 onward in North America) should have a clear green colour. The light green will darken with age – a brownish or dark tinge could indicate either a very dirty hydraulic system or possible fluid contamination. Lift the filter out of the reservoir (attached to the end of the hydraulic pump suction hose) and inspect it for debris and dirt.

Start the car and raise the suspension to its highest setting and, as the car continues to idle, inspect the undercarriage for evidence of hydraulic fluid. Don't crawl under the car (you are unfamiliar with this car and its hydraulic and suspension capabilities) but shine your flashlight along the rear suspension and underneath the drivetrain. Look for large wet spots and dripping.

Some leaks will show up only as the suspension lowers (forcing the hydraulic fluid to return to the hydraulic reservoir) so, while the car continues to idle, lower the suspension to its 'normal' driving height. Watch for any sudden fluid drips – especially at the rear of the front wheel wells and next to the rear wheels where the suspension return boots are located. Leaking return boots are not uncommon to the D so there is a good chance that you will find one – but not to worry, the boots are relatively inexpensive to replace (although the front boots do need the wings removed for access).

Note the hydraulic pump's recycling time while you continue to idle the car at its 'normal' suspension height. Listen for the click of the hydraulic regulator valve as it opens and closes. The click indicates that the hydraulic system has reached maximum pressure and the continuous stream of pressurized fluid, that the pump is still generating, is being redirected back to the hydraulic reservoir. Another click indicates that the pressure has dropped to a level that the system once again needs the pump to rebuild – thus a long time between pump cycles (20 seconds or more is considered acceptable) indicates a tight hydraulic system whereas lower cycle times are a sign of the system's inability to hold (a bad main accumulator) or retain the pressure (internal leaks somewhere in the hydraulic system).

Shut off the engine (don't step in and out of the car to activate the self-levelling) and watch for any drops in suspension height. A good tight suspension system should be able to maintain pressure for several hours; thus, a quick drop would indicate an internal leak in the suspension hydraulics. If the suspension does remain at its 'normal' height for an extended period test its ability to self-level while the engine is shut off – a push down on the front bumper should result in the car returning to its 'normal' height. The ability to do several of these push-raise combinations would indicate a very tight system. A poor test response is probably a sign of worn suspension cylinder seals – not an inexpensive repair.

Hydraulic pump

Inspect the pump for any leaks, especially below the pulley – if necessary, feel under the pulley for any dampness.

While the car is running, lower the suspension to its lowest setting (listen for the hissing to stop, indicating the release of hydraulic pressure) and then reset the suspension to its highest setting. Does the car rise quickly to its driving height (around 45 seconds)? Or does it labour to rebuild the pressure? If the suspension tested well (in the 'general' hydraulics suspension test) then an overlong period to raise the car is likely an indication of a worn hydraulic pump. The pump uses an aluminium piston body that could develop cracks, resulting in loss of ability to develop pressure. The pump can be rebuilt, preferably with a new aluminium body, although it will require a specialist to do so.

A close look at this hydraulic pump reveals a badly cracked pickup hose.

Pressure regulator and accumulators

The pressure regulator and main accumulator are mounted on the side of the engine below the intake manifold on all but the Citromatic DS EFi models, which have them mounted at the left front of the transmission. The pressure regulator is, in essence, the valve which regulates the amount of pressure that is fed into the hydraulic system and main accumulator. The main accumulator stores the reserve hydraulic pressure for the system. As a system, the regulator/accumulator combo is fairly foolproof – usually succumbing to leaks (either in the form of fluid or gas) rather than mechanical problems. Most of the older aluminium-body LHS2 regulators, which would sometimes crack, have already been replaced; thus, the regulators are mostly free of trouble other than an occasional worn valve ball or leaking seal. The gas-filled accumulator is a different story – it will typically lose pressure within 5-6 years, resulting in a drop in recycling time and sudden stiffness in the steering during hard cornering. Also inspect the pressure regulator return hose (you will need to use your flashlight), as the regulator's constant pressure spurts that are inflicted upon this hose make it a common area for hydraulic leaks. Finally, inspect the high pressure line from the hydraulic pump to the pressure regulator. The line needs to be secured at the centre of the bell housing and next to the pressure regulator – a sloppy installation, without proper securing, will result in eventual breakage.

Suspension

The suspension shocks – or rather spheres – are easy to check and almost as easy to replace. Idle the car in its 'normal' suspension height and push down on each corner – the suspension should give about 8in before resettling to its 'normal' height. Stiffness in the suspension indicates flat spheres that should be replaced at the earliest opportunity. Flat spheres negate any suspension travel and, in effect, transfer road shock directly to the chassis thereby causing frame stress and cracks. Fortunately, the front spheres can be replaced in minutes while the rear spheres, which are a little harder to access, take only marginally longer.

If you hear a clunk from the rear suspension as the car raises and lowers then a suspension ball seat is worn, causing the rod and ball to snap as the car changes height – they are not expensive but should be replaced as soon as possible as the worn seat could cause the suspension rod to break.

The pressure regulator/ accumulator is usually located below the intake manifold – it is mounted on the front of the transmission on the later injection DS.

Steering

Most of the cars will be equipped with hydraulically-assisted rack-and-pinion steering. Some of the ID and D Special cars will have manual non-hydraulic steering. The manual version, although simple and virtually problem-free, requires almost Popeye-sized arms to steer the car at slower speeds. On the other hand, the hydraulic steering, which requires more maintenance, is finger-light and a pleasure to use. Inspect the accordion boots for rips, and the steering rack for any visible fluid leaks. Check for an internal pressure leak on the power piston by turning the steering to a hard left or right lock – an increase in the hydraulic recycling time would indicate that

A leaking rear suspension return boot – a common D problem.

there is wear on the power piston or the piston seals. Constant hissing felt through the steering column would indicate worn rotating union seals. A binding feel during cornering may be due to a misaligned or improperly installed steering rack. A sudden stiffness or temporary loss of hydraulic assist in the steering is more likely to be a bad main accumulator.

Hydraulic lines and hoses

The hydraulic lines and hoses are the arteries of the hydraulic system. An untreated leak anywhere in the system will eventually affect every hydraulic component in the car. A low fluid level will result in the loss of hydraulic pressure causing the suspension to drop, the loss of braking and, on cars equipped with hydraulically-assisted steering and gear changing, steering to become difficult and gear changing gears impossible.

Inspect the condition of the steel lines – the lower lines in the engine bay, inside the left wheel wells and along the left frame sill, are the most susceptible to rust. Place the car in its highest suspension setting and use a flashlight to inspect inside the left rear mud guard (in front of the left rear wheel). A bundle of several hydraulic lines that run along the left frame sill are exposed to the outside elements and are the most likely areas for line rot.

Inspect some of the accessible hoses – they should not be too hard or too soft. Hard hoses will eventually develop cracks and soft hoses are a sign of either incorrect hose material or fluid contamination.

Brakes

Citroën brakes are hydraulically powered with front inboard rotors and rear drums. The brakes are highly effective and, once you become accustomed to them, you will sneer at conventional cars' brakes as mere pretenders.

Pull up the front floor mat to inspect for leaks from the brake pedal valve – an oily carpet is a sure sign that the brake valve boot is leaking.

Front brakes

The front brakes are mounted inboard and, although changing the pads is relatively simple, rebuilding the brake calipers or exchanging the rotors could be a full-day job. Inspect the condition of the brake pads – they should all be worn evenly – uneven pad wear could be an indication of sticking pistons. Run your finger along the edges of the brake rotor – there should be no lip on the edge or any grooves on the rotor's surface. Test the emergency brake – does it grip firmly? If the brake is ineffective and the emergency brake cannot be adjusted on the pad or the cable, you are faced with replacing the handbrake pads – a 6- to 8-hour job.

A leaking brake valve boot will soak the front mats with hydraulic fluid.

Rear brakes

The rear drum brakes see very little use as the large front brake rotors handle almost 80% of the braking. However, the brake shoes will wear eventually and need centring with a Citroën specific adjustment tool upon replacement. Also check the wheel cylinders for leaks (easy to spot on the inside

of the rear wheel) – especially on a LHS2 car – as a leaking cylinder will cause the shoes to bind and squeal.

The emergency brake calipers are hidden under the steering rack and are difficult to extract.

This front brake caliper shows almost new pads and no leaks.

Fuel systems   4 3 2 1

The carburetted versions of the D use either a single-barrel Solex (on all ID cars including the D Special) or a double-barrel Weber or Solex (on the DS and D Super) with the fuel supplied by a cam-driven mechanical fuel pump mounted on the left side of the engine. All cars have a 65-litre fuel tank (14.3 Imperial gallons – 17.2 US gallons) mounted directly below the rear passenger seat. The carburetted fuel systems are very reliable overall, although it might be necessary to clean the gas tank and/or the carburettor on cars that have had lengthy idle periods. If the carburettor does need replacement then it will be likely due to excessive play on the carb's main shaft caused by a worn accelerator-shaft hanger (mounted on the firewall directly behind the carb).

Fluid on the inside of this rear tyre is caused by a leaking brake cylinder.

The later EFi (electronic fuel injection) versions of the DS had electric pumps mounted at the right rear and are considered generally reliable – as long as they are well maintained. Inspect the fuel lines, hoses and wiring to ensure that they are in acceptable condition – a leaking or burst fuel line in the engine bay could result in a spectacular engine fire and the end of your beloved DS. Some injection parts are difficult to source so buying a DS EFi with missing injection components could lead to some long searches or larger-than-expected expenses.

Ignition and electrical   4 3 2 1

There were several different manufacturers of the D's ignition system, including SEV Marchal and Ducellier for the carburetted versions and Bosch for the later EFi cars. These distributors were manufactured with specific timing curves and advances for the D's different engine sizes, but are essentially interchangeable between all the different models – in fact, it is not unusual to see an ID distributor in a DS engine bay. Having said that, the D's ignition is a simple – albeit antiquated – system and, if the car runs reasonably well, you can assume that the car will only need a minor tune-up. Updating the distributor to electronic ignition is not frowned upon, even at car shows – so convert at the earliest opportunity and it will save considerably on future maintenance.

This worn carb shaft hanger will cause binding of the accelerator pedal, and wear the carb's main shaft.

Check overall wiring for splits and bare spots. The 1966 to 1969 cars suffer from bad rubberized insulation on the majority of the electrical wires in the harness, and are often a patchwork of different coloured

This mess of wiring is a typical botched repair on the 1966-69 D, which suffers from wire rot – fortunately, new wiring harnesses are available.

wires installed to replace bare ones in the engine bay. Unfortunately, these patchwork repairs usually do not extend to the equally bad wires under the dash – they will eventually short out or could even cause fires. Fortunately, a new electric harness can be bought for virtually every 1966 to 1969 model so replacing bad wiring is possible albeit at considerable cost. Installing a new harness will take a specialist about 20 hours – much longer if you do it.

Check the function of all the switches and electrical equipment – some electrical items are getting expensive to source (indicator switches from 1970 onward that double as the horn lever are almost impossible to find – even as a used part) or difficult to replace (the wiper motor's mounting bolts have to be accessed by removing the dashboard).

Charging and starting

From October 1967 onward, the D used an alternator with an external voltage regulator – the 1966 D still used a generator, although many of these earlier cars have now been converted to the much more efficient and smaller alternator. Listen for bearing noise from the alternator and inspect the battery for evidence of overcharging (white acid residue and low acid levels in the battery). If there do seem to be some charging issues be content in the knowledge that it is possible to replace the troublesome mechanical regulator with a more modern electronic one or, better yet, replace the original alternator with a modern lookalike that uses an internal voltage regulator.

There are two starter combinations on the 1966 to 1975 D – each with many variations. The earlier pre-1970 'large tooth' starter, mated to an equally 'large tooth' flywheel starter ring, will not interchange with the later 1970-on 'small tooth starter.' Although there are about ten different versions from two different manufacturers of the earlier starter, be aware that some of the repair parts are difficult to source, making a starter rebuild an expensive proposition. Not so for the later 'small tooth' starters – new reduction-gear starters are available that are higher cranking and considerably smaller than the OE unit. Whichever the combination, crank the starter several times to ensure that it engages properly and smoothly, as replacing the starter on some models could entail the time-consuming removal of the exhaust manifold (some of the later starters were compact enough to slip under the manifold).

In earlier cars, Citroën mounted the condensor in front of the D's radiator, but in 1972 these specially-designed AC condensors were mounted behind vented bumpers to alleviate chronic overheating.

Air conditioning

Although air conditioning systems were installed on the D prior to 1972, most were worthless as they caused chronic overheating. The problem with earlier AC systems was that the radiator-mounted condenser would reduce airflow to the barely adequate radiator – the compressor mounting was an afterthought and there was no secondary electrical fan. Citroën resolved all of these problems with the 1972 AC when it introduced a system utilizing the EFi's cross-flow radiator with an electric fan, modified the transmission bell housing to accept a beefy compressor mounting bracket and, most importantly, housed the condensers behind a vented front bumper.

If the car is equipped with this AC system then two wise upgrades would be a changeover to a rotary compressor instead of the OE piston compressor, and a freon upgrade from R12 to R134A.

Check the condition of the plastic underdash AC console, commonly used in US cars, as it decreases clearance for the passenger's knees and might have developed multiple cracks after years of knee banging (a replacement console would be difficult to find). The last of the European AC-equipped cars had a more practical centre console that eliminated knee banging.

Wheel bearings and axles

Wheel bearings are not a common wear item on the D – most last the lifetime of the car. If there is a bearing noise from the wheels, assume that water somehow got to the bearings.

The axles are almost as durable as the bearings – at least compared to most other front-wheel-drive cars – but a lack of regular greasing, combined with torn axle boots, can drastically reduce life expectancy. You will test the axles during the test drive phase.

Ball joints

Each front wheel hub has an upper and lower ball joint that allows the hub to swivel on the suspension arms. Because of the suspension arm layout, the upper ball joint receives a minimal amount of stress and, as a result, rarely wears. The lower ball joint, however, even if regularly greased and well maintained, will eventually wear. You will test the ball joints during the test drive phase.

Front suspension arms

Stand in front of the car and check the upright stance of the front tyres. There are no camber or caster adjustments to the front wheels so if one or both of the tyres stand at an odd angle, expect a suspension arm problem. The suspension arms (typically the lower one) can bend with violent angled collisions against the curb or a pothole. An angled wheel cannot be adjusted straight unless a Citroën specialist, using a Citroën measuring tool, is willing to tap it back with a sledgehammer. This will work in some cases but you are more likely to be confronted with an expensive arm replacement.

The suspension arms are mounted in aluminium assemblies that are bolted to tubes welded on the frame. The tube welds can develop stress cracks (mostly from driving with bad front suspension spheres) and reveal themselves as a violent vibration or shimmy at higher speeds. Such a shimmy or vibration should merit further inspection by a Citroën specialist as the repair could be extremely expensive.

Engine

The D's 4-cylinder 5-main-bearing has a well-deserved robust reputation. Well-maintained engines are known to have survived for 250,000+ miles without needing extensive repairs. But like any other engine, the D engine will not survive long-term

Check the front stance of the car for odd-angled wheels which would indicate a suspension arm problem. Jeff Meyer's 1972 DS21 checks out fine.

Underneath the panel inside the front wheel well is the front suspension arm assembly. The accordion suspension return boot is a common source of hydraulic leaks.

abuse or poor maintenance. Listen for rod-knock when the engine is cold (before oil pressure is built up) and when the engine is hot (when the oil is thinner). Check the aluminium cylinder head for seepage at the block joint as that could indicate a warping problem. Check under the exhaust manifold for overheating or freezing – look for coolant and rust trails snaking down the block. Does the oil pressure light flicker at idle? – this could be caused by a poor oil pressure switch but more likely is an indication of low oil pressure, caused by either worn engine bearings or an oil pump problem (note: the oil filter is mounted directly in the oil pump and a clogged filter or incorrect filter installation would cause oil pressure loss).

Remove and inspect the oil-filler cap. The oil on the cap might be black but should not be gunky – a whitish 'milkshake' layer on the oil cap indicates water in the oil and, depending how long it's been there, probable water damage to many inner metal components.

Pull the dipstick and inspect the oil level. Is it excessively high? If so, the fuel pump might be leaking into the engine and mixing fuel with the oil – this will cause poor lubrication, damage the engine bearings and, if left untreated, cause eventual engine seizure. Smell the dipstick to confirm any fuel presence.

Pop loose the three air filter clamps and inspect inside the air filter housing. If there is any oil inside the housing then excessive pressure, caused by bad piston rings, is bringing up oil from the bottom of the engine through the blow-by hose. Blue smoke from the tailpipe would confirm this.

Listen for tappet noise – the valves are easily adjusted, but excessive tappet noise could be caused by a worn camshaft or lifters.

Ask for the car's service history – this might be the only available means to determine if a timing chain replacement is indicated in the near future. The chain can last as long as 150,000 miles on the 1911cc ID19 engine – however, the chain's life expectancy decreases as the engine size increases – a DS23 or AC-equipped car can expect only about 100,000 to 120,000 miles from a chain. An excessively worn chain can be felt by checking the play on the main pulley but otherwise there is no way to gauge the chain's condition. Replacing the timing chain can only be done by removing the car's entire drivetrain – a 14-hour job on an ID and a 22-hour job on a Citromatic DS EFi.

The water contamination in this valve cover can usually be seen by inspecting the oil cap.

Engine balance

	Ex	Gd	Av	Po
	4	3	2	1

It might not be possible, during this inspection, to check engine compression, but a quick 'balance' test might help

The timing chain can only be replaced by removing the entire drivetrain.

This chain is almost entirely worn, as can be seen by inspecting the tensioner – chain wear is difficult to discern while the engine is still in the car.

This engine mount would be very noisy as the metal shell is touching the engine bracket.

identify a weak cylinder. Pull the plug wires and refit them loosely in the distributor cap, start the engine and remove one wire at a time, thereby running the car on 3 cylinders (a rubber glove would come in handy here to insulate your hand while removing and re-installing the plug wires). There should be a noticeable rpm drop but the engine should continue to run – the rpm drop should be fairly even on all 4 cylinders. A small or no drop in rpm could indicate a bad spark plug or wire, but could also indicate low compression on that particular cylinder. Further investigation of the spark plug and a compression check might be in order before committing to the purchase of the car.

Engine smoke

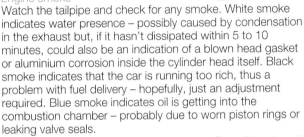

Watch the tailpipe and check for any smoke. White smoke indicates water presence – possibly caused by condensation in the exhaust but, if it hasn't dissipated within 5 to 10 minutes, could also be an indication of a blown head gasket or aluminium corrosion inside the cylinder head itself. Black smoke indicates that the car is running too rich, thus a problem with fuel delivery – hopefully, just an adjustment required. Blue smoke indicates oil is getting into the combustion chamber – probably due to worn piston rings or leaking valve seals.

Engine mounts

The rubber metal-encased engine mounts on the D are placed directly below the exhaust and intake manifolds. The exhaust-side engine mount is more likely to fail due to its proximity to heat and the engine's torque direction. On the exhaust side, you can reach under the mount bracket and feel if any of the rubber has collapsed through the bottom – indicating a worn mount. If the mount has totally failed then the bracket connecting the engine mount to the engine will be resting on the mount's metal casing. Checking the intake side mount is a slightly harder task as room is tight but, using a flashlight, you can inspect the height of the mount and compare it to the exhaust side. Failed mounts will present themselves an engine vibration or, if they are totally collapsed, a loud rumble during acceleration.

Transmission

The front-wheel-drive manual-shift transmission will be either four or five speed. The five-speed version was also available as an 'overdrive-5' or 'close-ratio-5.' The 'overdrive-5' transmission, common to the DS21 and DS23, and identical to the transmission used in the Citroën SM, uses a higher geared fifth gear whereas the 'close-ratio-5' has a final gear that is closer to the 4-speed transmission in its final drive. Like the engine, the transmission is fairly robust. However, poor shifting habits can lead to synchro ring damage, and high mileage will eventually wear the transmission bearings. It is expensive to repair a worn transmission and a more economical alternative would be to find a good used lower mileage unit.

Citromatic transmission

4 3 2 1

The 4-speed Citromatic transmission is a lot more reliable than some critics give it credit for. Citromatic problems are more likely to be due to improper adjustment than an internal mechanical problem. Several adjustments have to be done precisely and in specific sequence in order for the system to work correctly.

The compact all-in-one transmission, differential, brake rotors, brake calipers and hydraulic shift cover of a Citromatic DS23.

Also, check the centrifugal regulator (mounted above the hydraulic pump) for leaks and worn mounting bushings.

Finally, an unusual problem that could plague the Citromatic system is loss of hydraulic fluid through the transmission shift cover – the shift cover has a series of pistons with seals that could fail and leak hydraulic fluid into the transmission. A sure sign of such a leak is loss of hydraulic fluid without any apparent leaks – this can be verified by checking the transmission which will probably reveal an excessively high level of thinned-out oil.

The centrifugal regulator is an integral part of the DS Citromatic hydraulics. Check for play in the bearings and mounting bushings.

Automatic transmission

4 3 2 1

It's unlikely you will be considering one of these as not many were manufactured. The transmission is a modified version of the Borg Warner T35 – a relatively decent transmission providing it is maintained. However, the transmission is not easy to rebuild – even by an 'automatic' specialist – so if the transmission is worn or problematic you might be wise to reconsider your purchase.

Evidence of ATF oil in the differential (checked with a dipstick located between the transmission and engine) indicates a leaking pinion shaft seal. Low pressure in the transmission oil pump will cause a shudder while reversing the car. Check that the ATF fluid is red and clear, remove the dipstick (behind the radiator cooling fans) and smell the ATF for a burning odour that would indicate burnt and/or slipping friction plates.

Clutch replacement is a time-consuming repair on a D – especially on an AC-equipped Citromatic DS.

Clutch

4 3 2 1

Check the adjustment on the clutch fork – if it is about halfway along the adjustment rod, the clutch is reaching the end of its usable life. A clutch replacement will take a minimum of 12 hours (on the simpler ID versions) and as long as 18 hours (on the Citromatic DS with AC). You will check the clutch for slippage during the test drive phase.

Test drive

You are now ready to take the car on a test drive of at least 15 minutes – a test that should include a variation of road surfaces and speeds. The different surfaces and speeds are needed to test the condition and reaction of the suspension, steering, brakes, ball joints, axles, transmission and clutch.

Make sure that you are familiar with all of the switches and have the seat and mirrors adjusted to your satisfaction so that you can concentrate on the car's performance.

Ex Gd Av Po
4 3 2 1

Engine

Listen for a rod-knock during initial startup and again when the car warms up. Look in the mirror and check for any smoke during acceleration and deceleration. Is there any engine vibration or rumbling as you accelerate which would indicate worn mounts? Does the car run smoothly without any hiccups as you accelerate?

Ex Gd Av Po
4 3 2 1

Transmission

Listen for any transmission bearing noise. Also check the condition of the second and third synchro rings by downshifting into these gears at about 2000rpm. A grinding complaint as you downshift indicates a worn synchro – a very expensive repair, probably requiring a specialist.

Ex Gd Av Po
4 3 2 1

Citromatic transmission

The gears should engage smoothly as you shift from one to the next. A hesitation or an abrupt shift will probably mean just an adjustment of the settings. An increase in rpm without an equal response in movement is a clutch problem. Remember – only shift between first and reverse gear while at a dead stop as doing so otherwise will force the hydraulic gear change to shift it into gear with possible catastrophic consequences.

Ex Gd Av Po
4 3 2 1

Clutch

The clutch pedal should grab at about half depression and engage without jerking. If a hill is present, try to pull way up the hill from a dead stop – engine revving with little or no movement from the car is a sure sign of a worn clutch. Also check the clutch at higher speeds by suddenly accelerating in fourth gear; an increase in rpm without an increase in speed would indicate a worn clutch disc.

Ex Gd Av Po
4 3 2 1

Brakes

A minimal amount of effort should be required to engage the brakes. A single hesitation when first applying the brakes is probably due to a flat brake accumulator – continuous hesitation in the brakes is caused by either air in the brakes or a sticking brake caliper piston. A single stuck brake caliper will cause the car to pull under harder braking situations – if the car pulls to the right then the left caliper is sticking, and vice versa. A strange pulsating feel in the brake pedal could be due to either worn and/or warped brake rotors, or pad wear grooves in the aluminium brake caliper housings.

Suspension

Ex Gd Av Po
4 3 2 1

The hydraulic suspension should be able to cope with major potholes and road bumps at speeds in excess of 30mph. If the car's suspension reacts violently at lower speeds and smaller bumps then a change of suspension spheres is in order. Don't test the car at the higher speed until you have done some lower speed tests.

If possible, check the car's performance at highway speeds. A violent shaking or vibration at this speed could indicate cracked suspension arm nuts or loose suspension arm assemblies. Such shaking will require further investigation as the cost to repair these deficiencies will be exorbitant.

Steering

Ex Gd Av Po
4 3 2 1

As you drive at slow speed, check for an internal leak on the power piston by turning the steering to a hard left or right lock – an increase in hydraulic recycling time would indicate that there is wear at the centre of the power piston or on the power piston seals. A sudden stiffness or temporary loss of hydraulic assist in the steering is more likely to be due to a bad main accumulator.

Axles

Ex Gd Av Po
4 3 2 1

To test the condition of the axle joints, make hard left and right turns at slow speeds and listen for any clacking sounds – which could indicate either a worn outer axle joint or tri-ax housing. Well-used axles and housings, albeit not cheap, are plentiful, so assume you have a bad combination of both and negotiate the purchase price accordingly.

Ball joints

Ex Gd Av Po
4 3 2 1

To test the ball joints, drive the car slowly over a pothole or speed bump. A worn ball joint will complain with an obvious knocking sound, which will get louder with increased wear, and excessively worn ball joints have been known to break loose from the hub. Assume that replacement rather than greasing of the ball joints will be necessary.

Rattles and wind noise

Ex Gd Av Po
4 3 2 1

Listen for rattles and wind noise. Rattles from a door are probably worn window guides or winder mechanisms. Wind noise from a door window might also be worn window guides, but could be a bad adjustment of the door's front and rear window channels or door hinges. Wind noise from the bottom of the doors might necessitate further inspection of the lower frame sills – a previous side impact in an accident might be causing sealing problems. Wind noise around the windscreen and top of the dashboard is probably due to just a poorly installed windscreen, but check the windscreen frame to make sure that rust isn't causing a sealing problem.

Evaluation procedure

Add up the total points score: 280 = excellent, possibly concours; 210 = good; 140 = average; 70 = poor. Cars scoring over 196 should be completely usable, requiring only routine maintenance and care to be kept in good condition. Cars scoring between 70 and 142 will probably require a full restoration. Those scoring between 143 and 195 will need a very careful assessment of the work necessary, and its cost, in order to reach a realistic valuation.

10 Auctions
– sold! Another way to buy your dream

There are two types of auctions that might feature a Citroën D-model: a disposal auction, where dealers or garages sell off their unwanted inventory or repossessed vehicles, or a classic car auction, where you are more likely to find a restored or excellent low-mileage, one-owner car, albeit at a much higher price. You're more likely to find a bargain in the first scenario but a better car in the second one.

Auction pros and cons
Pros: Prices are typically lower as dealers and resellers, unwilling to pay too much for their purchases, often frequent these auctions. Auctioneers typically guarantee clear title.
Cons: There will be very little opportunity for an in-depth inspection and you will be unable to drive the car. Sometimes all that will be available to you, before you make your decision, is an inadequate description in an auction catalogue.

Which auction?
Classic car auctions can be found in car magazines whereas 'disposal' auctions, which are held more frequently, are sometimes listed in phone directories. A search on the internet will probably find either one and, once found, the auctioneer's website will probably list if any Citroën D-models will be featured in upcoming auctions. If the website details past auctions then peruse them to see if previous buyers got bargains or overpaid.

Catalogue and payment details
The catalogue or website will usually detail price estimates for the auction vehicles, auction charges and payment methods. Most auctions will require an immediate and sizeable deposit and that the remaining balance to be paid within 24 hours. Cash (to a certain extent) or bank drafts are usually required as auction companies are unlikely to want to absorb the associated costs of credit card payments or the risk of a personal cheque.

Viewing
Most auctions offer a 'viewing' period, usually the day before or the morning of the auction, when potential buyers can view the cars. The 'viewing' period will allow you to inspect the engine bay and passenger compartment without the opportunity of driving the car. Since most auction entrance fees allow you to bring a guest, and auction staff will typically start a car for you if asked, invite along a mechanic or a mechanically-minded friend. Their ability to inspect the engine bay and listen for unusual sounds could save you from a financial headache.

Buyer's premium
In the case of classic car auctions, the final bidding price (also known as the hammer price) does not include the auction house's buyer's premium. This premium is usually percentage of the hammer price. Remember to factor in this additional cost, and any state and/or county taxes, to the amount you are willing to pay.

Bidding
Auctions can be very exciting and it is in the auction house's best interest to get potential buyers swept up in a bidding frenzy on a vehicle. This rarely results in a bargain for the eventual buyer so the caveat at an auction is 'set a price you are willing to pay and stick to it.'

   If you are unfamiliar with how an auction works arrive well before your car goes on the block and observe the proceedings. Once your car is up for auction place an early bid – this will let the auctioneer know that you are an interested bidder and he will continue to look to you for any higher bids. If you do win the auction you will be directed to an accounting section and given a total (including any buyer's premium and taxes) and required to make an immediate deposit – you will also probably make further arrangements for paying the balance and picking up the car. If the car is unsold in the auction leave contact information with the auctioneer in case the seller is willing to accept your final bid.

Successful bid
Once the car is paid for the objective is to get it home. A call to your insurance company will be necessary if you are able to drive it, otherwise you will need to arrange for either a trailer or the services of a transportation company. (The auction house can probably recommend several suitable transportation firms if necessary.) Make sure that the transportation company is familiar with the D-model's hydraulic suspension, and that the car has to be secured in its lowest position to prevent damage during transport.

eBay and internet auctions
I'm told that some bargains can be found through eBay and other internet auction sites, but my personal experience is such that I find this the least preferred method of purchase. Internet sellers, even those with the best intentions, will typically concentrate on the car's positives and gloss over its flaws. Even the most detailed pictures can be deceiving about the car's actual condition so try and inspect the car in person if at all possible. If you absolutely must have the featured eBay car try to bid no more than 75% of what you think the car is worth because, in my experience, there will be several disappointments and undisclosed repairs to deal with.

Auctioneers
Barrett Jackson	www.barrett-jackson.com
Bonhams	www.bonhams.com
Christies	www.christies.com
Coys	www.coys.co.uk
eBay	www.motors.ebay.com
H&H	www.classic-auctions.co.uk
Sweet Chariots	
(list of auction events)	www.sweetchariots.com

11 Paperwork
– correct documentation is essential!

The paper trail
Classic, collector and prestige cars usually come with a large collection of paperwork, collected and passed on from owner to owner. This documentation represents the actual history of the car and from it can be deduced the level of care it has received, the frequency of use, which specialists have worked on it, and the dates and mileage of major repairs and restorations. All of this information will be invaluable to you as the new owner, so be very wary of cars with little paperwork to support their claimed history.

Registration documents
All countries/states have some form of registration for private vehicles, whether it's like the American 'pink slip' system or the British 'log book' system.

It is essential to check that the registration document is genuine, that it relates to the car in question, and that all the vehicle's details, including the VIN, are correctly recorded. If you are buying directly from the previous owner then his or her name and address will be recorded in the document: this will not be the case if you are buying from a dealer.

In the UK the current (Euro-aligned) registration document is the 'V5C', which is printed in coloured sections of blue, green and pink. The blue section relates to the car specification, the green section has details of the new owner, and the pink section is sent to the DVLA in the UK when the car is sold.

In the UK the DVLA will provide details of earlier owners of the vehicle upon payment of a small fee, and much can be learned in this way.

Continental or USA paperwork may be more expensive and time-consuming to complete. Is that something you want to deal with?

Roadworthiness certificate
Most country/state administrations require that vehicles are regularly tested to prove that they are safe to use on the public highway and do not produce excessive emissions. In the UK that test (the MoT) is carried out, for a fee, at approved testing stations. In the USA, the requirement varies from state to state, but most insist on an emissions test every two years. Many states, including California, have exemption ages (currently 1974 and older cars are exempt from smog) while the police are charged with pulling over unsafe-looking vehicles.

In the UK the test is required on an annual basis once a vehicle becomes three years old. Of particular relevance for older cars is that the certificate issued includes the mileage reading recorded at the test date and, therefore, becomes an independent record of that car's history. Ask the seller if previous certificates are available. Without an MoT or registration, the vehicle will need to be towed home, although you could insist that a valid MoT is part of the purchase. (This is not a bad idea as you will then know that the car was roadworthy on the day it was tested.)

Road license
The administration of every country/state charges some kind of tax for the use of

its road system. The actual form of the 'road license' and how it is displayed varies enormously from country to country and state to state.

Whatever the form of the 'road license', it must relate to the vehicle carrying it and must be present and valid if the car is to be legally driven on the public highway. In the UK, if a car is untaxed because it has not been used for a period of time, the owner has to inform the licensing authorities, otherwise the vehicle's date-related registration number will be lost and there will be a painful amount of paperwork to get it re-registered. Also in the UK, vehicles built before the end of 1972 are provided with 'tax discs' free of charge, but they must still display a valid disc. Car clubs can often provide formal proof that a particular car qualifies for this valuable concession.

Certificates of authenticity

For many makes of collectible car it is possible to get a certificate proving the age and authenticity (e.g. engine and chassis numbers, paint colour and trim) of a particular vehicle; these are sometimes called 'Heritage Certificates' and if the car comes with one of these it is a definite bonus. If you want to obtain one, the relevant owners club is the best starting point.

Valuation certificate

Hopefully, the vendor will have a recent valuation certificate, or letter signed by a recognized expert stating how much they believe the car to be worth (such documents, together with photos, are usually needed to get 'agreed value' insurance). Generally, these documents should act only as confirmation of your own assessment of the car rather than a guarantee of value as the expert has probably not actually seen the vehicle. The easiest way to find out how to obtain a formal valuation is to contact the owners club.

Service history

Many cars will have been serviced by the owner rather than a specialist – possibly for a good number of years. Nevertheless, try to obtain as much service history and other paperwork pertaining to the car as you can. Recognized speciality garage receipts are the most preferred. However, any paperwork will help: items like the original bill of sale, sales brochure, handbook, parts invoices and repair bills, will add to the story and character of the car. If the seller claims that the car has been restored, ask for receipts and other evidence from a specialist restorer.

If the seller claims to have carried out regular servicing, ask what, where and when – hopefully, with some evidence backing up the claims. Your assessment of the car's overall condition should tell you whether the seller's claims are genuine.

Restoration photographs

If the seller tells you that the car has been restored, expect to be shown a series of photographs taken during the restoration. Pictures taken at various stages, and from various angles, should help you gauge the thoroughness of the work. If you buy the car, ask if you can have all the photographs as they form an important part of the vehicle's history. It's surprising how many sellers are happy to part with their car and accept your cash, but want to hang on to their photographs! In the latter event, you may be able to persuade the seller to get a set of copies made.

12 What's it worth to you?
– let your head rule your heart!

This centre-mounted AC console was offered on late Euro-market cars only.

Having worked through the previous chapters while inspecting the car, you should now have an good idea of the car's condition. Is the car a restoration project? If so, unless that was your purchase goal, you might want to walk away. Or is the car a well-maintained driver with minor issues? – issues that you hopefully found during your inspection and should now be able to use in haggling over the price. Like most classic cars, mechanical and cosmetic conditions are not the sole factors in determining the car's sale price; rarity and desirability are also major considerations. A ratty Chapron-built DS21 Prestige would still fetch more than an immaculate late-1960s ID19.

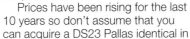

A correct factory radio as mounted in a later 1970 onward dashboard.

Newer cars, especially DS23 models, typically are pricier than equal condition older cars, thus keep in mind that you could probably buy a near-pristine ID for the price of a worn DS23 EFi.

Prices have been rising for the last 10 years so don't assume that you can acquire a DS23 Pallas identical in price and condition to that your buddy bought several years ago. Educate yourself about the car's relative value. Invest in some classic car magazines that publish price guides. Check car dealers' websites for similar cars and their asking prices. Call a Citroën D specialist and ask about current values and sales prices – most will be willing to talk to you, especially if they view you as a potential client. All of this will help you to establish whether your purchase is of fair value or overpriced.

These Jaeger gauges are a hard-to-find aftermarket option for the earlier, sloped dashboards.

Desirable extras

The post-1971 factory air conditioning with the air-vented bumpers is much sought-after and could add considerably to the car's purchase price if in good working order. Electronic ignition, although unoriginal, makes the car more reliable and is an accepted add-on. Valance-mounted driving lights are quite rare, although susceptible to damage as they are mounted below the bumper and outside of the rubber guards. The extra set of driving lights on the 1966 D, especially the teardrop-shaped version, is also very sought-after. Not a lot of wheel and hubcap options were offered on the car other than some Chapron-designed faux wire caps and a smattering of other D-specific hubcaps.

These side mouldings were a rare and briefly offered factory option.

The desirable and hard-to-find sunroof – this one is installed on a 1975 DS23.

The optional teardrop driving lights are an attractive option on this 1966 DS21.

Very little has been made available in the way of dress-up trim, although Citroën did briefly offer a pricey, gold-coloured moulding set, and aftermarket companies still sell Citroën-specific bonnet handles.

Stainless steel exhaust systems are very desirable and preferred for cars in damp climates. Factory-installed radios can also add to the car's value, especially on the later round-dial cars, as the radio's location, in the centre of the dash, is extremely small and not suitably sized for aftermarket radios.

The rarest option is probably the steel panel sunroof – very few of these were installed due to the difficulty and cost of fitting them in the D-model's fibreglass roof.

Undesirable features

Some cars had dealer-installed or aftermarket air conditioning systems. Almost without exception, these systems are garbage. The installation typically included a condenser mounted in front of the radiator, which reduced airflow to the cooling system, thereby causing chronic overheating. Also included was a compressor, attached to the engine with inadequate flimsy brackets and driven by the original waterpump, which caused excessive vibration and regular waterpump failure.

One of the few wheel or hubcap options for the D.

Because aftermarket radios don't fit the original placement, many are installed by cutting into the dash. Non-specialists, who would frequently cut into the door frames and even the frame walls to place speakers, installed a lot of these radios. The dashboard would have to be replaced if you wanted to restore to original spec.

Cheap paintjobs and interiors which have been re-upholstered in bad taste should drastically lower your purchase offer as the money you might be spending in the future to correct these deficiencies could be very considerable.

Striking a deal

Keep in mind that you are buying an older classic car. If doubtful about any aspect of the car it would be prudent to get an independent mechanical check – preferably by a knowledgeable specialist. Otherwise, if you think the price accurately reflects the car's condition or, even better, the price represents a bargain, then it is time to strike a deal. If the seller has done his homework and knows the price is fair, you might not be able to easily haggle him down. Use any defects that you found during the chapter 9 inspections to justify a discount.

This 1969 DS21 dash has one of the earlier 'junk' AC consoles.

Most buyers will either be searching for high quality cars or more moderately priced cars that might need some work but could easily be daily drivers. It is unlikely that many buyers will be lined up to purchase the less attractive 'restorable' or 'basket case' cars. However, if you are actually considering such a vehicle, either because you are a hobbyist or you want to build a car over time and on a budget, then keep several things in mind:

Restorable or basket case?
There is a fine line between what some people consider a restorable car and what others regard as a basket case. Poor condition cars can run the gamut from badly maintained rusty vehicles

A close inspection should determine whether this car has 'restoration' or 'parts car' potential.

to ones that have been standing among the weeds in someone's backyard for 20 years. Even if you are paying a relatively insignificant amount of money for a car, you will still need to educate yourself about the full extent of the work needed. Buy the wrong car and you could be well into the restoration before realising that you are restoring a worthless pile of junk. Rust is probably the deciding factor as to whether the vehicle is a 'parts' car or worth considering for restoration. Your priority should be to inspect the chassis very carefully – rusty body panels can be replaced, and

the mechanicals – no matter how poor the condition – will probably be replaced or renewed.

Do it yourself or hire a specialist?
So, you have decided that you want to buy a decrepit Citroën that you intend to rebuild and finish to your liking. Do you have the mechanical skill needed to tackle the Citroën's complex hydraulics, and, if not, a sizeable bank account to keep a specialist working at a steady rate? What will you be capable of doing yourself? Do you have enough mechanical knowledge to tackle the drivetrain overhaul or hydraulic refurbishment? Are you equipped to deal

A ratty engine but functional and complete engine bay – probably a good restoration candidate.

with the electrics or necessary body work? Some people have the patience and skill necessary to tackle body work but lack the knowledge necessary for mechanical or electrical refurbishment. Take stock of your own skills as these will decide where and when you will need the assistance of specialists. If your plan is to hire a specialist for the entire restoration process, keep in mind that the cost of restoration will heavily outweigh the finished car's value.

This sad Cabriolet was stored away and shows the ravages of neglect.

Document everything

If your plan is to do some of the 'tear down' work yourself, take care to document everything carefully. A restoration could span several years so those bolts and bits that you are intimately familiar with on the day of removal could have you scratching your head several years later, wondering where they go. If you are de-trimming the car for the body shop, tape or box items together for specific body parts. If you are removing mechanical components and dropping them off at the specialist for refurbishment, videotape or photograph the removal process to help with eventual correct placement and re-installment.

Do you have the resources?

In addition to a well-equipped toolbox and workbench, you will also need the funds to maintain a steady flow of necessary new parts and pay for work done by specialists. An unprepared or inadequate budget can turn a well-intended one year restoration into a neverending messy nightmare, cluttering up your garage.

If you have the tools and the budget, keep in mind that you will need a sizeable garage with plenty of room to manoeuvre around the car, and sufficient space to store the removed parts. Finally and most importantly, a patient and supportive partner is a must – nothing kills a restoration faster than a fed up 'other half' demanding immediate removal of 'that pile of crap' in the garage.

14 Paint problems
– bad complexion, including dimples, pimples and bubbles

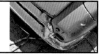

Paint problems are usually due to either bad maintenance or a poor respray. Look for some of the following signs:

Orange peel
An effect caused by too much paint having been applied to the body surface, giving an orange peel texture to the paint. This can sometimes be remedied by wet sanding and buffing the paint. Care should be taken in this process as over-sanding could cause thin and light spots. This is also very labour intensive and could be expensive if you choose a professional to do it.

Fading
Some colours, especially reds, are very susceptible to fading from sun exposure. The paint can sometimes be brought back with cutting compounds and waxing – if this fails then a repaint is the only recourse.

Crazing/cracking
Caused by poor preparation of the paint surface or a reaction between the upper layer of paint and a previous layer of paint or prep material. Probably happened because of a cheaper paintjob when a shortcut was used to repaint the car. The only solution is to take the surface back to bare metal and repaint.

This boot lid shows bad prep work from an older paint job – the plastic filler is up to ½in thick in some areas.

Bubbling
This is due to rust forming under the paint. The only satisfactory remedy is to remove the paint, treat or cut out the rust, possibly replace some sheet metal and repaint the affected area.

Micro blistering
Usually caused by poor preparation of a paintjob – either condensation got into the primer before the paint was applied, or a solvent was trapped under the paint. Could also be caused by cheaper car covers that lack breathing ability. The only solution is to repaint the affected area.

Clouding/peeling
Frequently caused by a poorly applied or sun-damaged clear coat. Usually the clear coat can be re-applied over the existing paintjob.

Dimples
Dimples in the paintwork are usually caused by large patches of wax or silicone left on the bodywork before respraying. Frequently found on inexpensive paintjobs where little care is taken with body preparation. The paint must be removed and reapplied on affected areas.

Small dents
Small 'car-parking' dents can frequently be cured by dent specialists, who can often remove the dent without the need for body work or repainting the dented area. They are usually mobile so check your local telephone directory for someone who can come to your home or place of business to repair the dent. This is not always successful with the large aluminium bonnet or the lower quarter of the doors or fenders (where secondary layers of sheet metal could be affected).

15 Problems due to lack of use
– just like their owners, D-models need exercise!

Hydraulic fluid problems
The earlier LHS hydraulic system (pre-1967 on non-USA cars and prior to mid-1969 on USA cars) is vegetable-based (like a non-Citroën's brake fluid) and will absorb water causing internal rust problems. Unlike most conventional cars, the Citroën D model's hydraulic system also powers the suspension, steering and, on Citromatic cars, the shifting – a contaminated hydraulic system can be a catastrophic problem. If an LHS car has been unused for an extended period, expect seized brake calipers and cylinders, and possible internal damage in the steering and suspension cylinders.

The later LHM mineral-based hydraulic system is not nearly as problematic, although expect sticking brake calipers and rear cylinders after extended inactivity.

Suspension problems
The suspension spheres (one at each wheel) and accumulators (main hydraulic on all and brake accumulator for the DS version) will lose their gas quicker on inactive cars. Flat spheres will give the car a harsh ride and deflated accumulators will cause short hydraulic recycling times. Fortunately, spheres and accumulators are relatively inexpensive and easy to replace.

Engine problems
Examine the dipstick and oil cap – light-coloured is a good sign, black is obviously old, sludge is a sign of poor maintenance and a white 'mayonnaise' sludge on the oil cap is a sign of water contamination. Engine inactivity could cause several problems including sticking piston rings (which could break when the engine is turned over or started) and condensation contamination on internal metal components such as the crankshaft and engine bearings.

Clutch problems
The clutch could stick if unused for a lengthy period. Typically, this resolves itself once the engine has run for a while and the clutch pedal is repeatedly depressed – however, in some cases the clutch plate will fail entirely which would necessitate removal of the transmission and replacement of the clutch assembly.

Coolant problems
Old antifreeze or plain tap water can play havoc with the D-model's aluminium cylinder head and waterpump. In extreme cases, corrosion inside the cylinder head could cause the coolant to enter the head's oil passages and, therefore, the oil sump. Remove the radiator cap (on cars without coolant expansion tanks) and examine the radiator tubes – inactivity in the cooling system will accelerate radiator clogs and excessive hardened clogging will require radiator core replacement.

Tyres
It is likely that a car stored for an extended period will have flat, deformed or deteriorated tyres. Tyres have a finite shelf life, which shortens under sun exposure.

Corrosion and rot, as seen on this boot ledge, will set in if the car is not stored properly.

Aluminium corrosion will attack many of the engine components, including the alternator and water pump.

Excessive cracking in the tyres' sidewall will require immediate tyre replacement to prevent a potential blowout.

Rubber hoses
Hoses in both hydraulic and coolant systems are susceptible to age and prolonged idle periods. Cracks and splits in either systems' hoses could result in total fluid loss – typically at the most inopportune time.

Body rubbers
Door window, boot and roof seals can crack due to sun exposure and allow water to enter the doors, boot and passenger compartment.

Electricals
The electrical system does not react kindly to underuse. The battery will be flat and need replacement; corrosion will attack electrical connections, and the alternator and starter might have flat spots, sticking brushes or internal corrosion.

Ignition problems
The ignition system is also susceptible to corrosion and disuse problems – the leaf points could corrode and break, the distributor cap brush could stick, causing contact problems, spark plug wires could deteriorate causing ineffective sparks, and the spark plug tips could corrode resulting in an equally weak spark.

Rotting exhaust system
Water will collect in the exhaust system from atmospheric condensation – if the car is left unused, without the opportunity for the exhaust to heat up and evaporate the water, expect rust holes in the lowest portions (where water will collect) of the muffler, resonator and connecting pipes.

Greasing points
The suspension arms, ball joints and driveshafts have several greasing nipples that should be regreased during service intervals. If the car is unused the grease will harden and lose its ability to lubricate, resulting in component damage.

Gasoline problems
A D-model that has been stored for 12 months or more could probably benefit from carb cleaning and fuel filter replacement. Storage periods of even longer could cause the gasoline to gel in the gas tank and require the tank to be cleaned and fuel pump replaced.

16 The Community
– key people, organizations and companies in the Citroën D world

UK clubs
Citroën Car Club,
PO Box 348, Steyning, West Sussex,
BN44 3XN
www.citroencarclub.org.uk
e-mail: members@citroencarclub.org.uk

European clubs
Denmark
Dansk ID & DS Club
www.idds.dk

France
DS ID Club of France
13/17 Aubry City, 75020, Paris
www.dsidclubdefrance.net
e-mail: dsidclubfrance@yahoo.fr

Federation des Clubs Ideale DS,
148 rue Marel Cachin, 37700,
Saint Pierre des Corps
www.ideale-ds.com

Germany
DS Club Deutschland
www.dsclub.de

Italy
IDeeSse ID D & DS Club
www.riasc.it/IDeeSse

The Netherlands
Citroën Club Nederland
www.citroenclubnederland.nl

Citroën ID/DS Club Nederland
www.citroeniddsclub.nl

Norway
Citroën ID/DS Club Norway
www.dsid.no

Sweden
Svenska Citroën Klubben
www.citroenklubben.com

Overseas
Australia
CCOCA
www.citroenclassic.org.au

Citroën Car Club of New South Wales
www.citroencarclub.org.au

Canada
Citroën Autoclub Canada
www.citroenautoclub.ca

Ottawa Citroën Club
www.ottawacitroenclub.ca

New Zealand
Citroën Car Club of New Zealand
www.citroencarclubnz.freeyellow.com

USA
Citroën Car Clubs
www.citroenclubsusa.org

Citroën Club of America
www.citroen-ca.com

San Francisco Region CCC
www.citroensanfrancisco.com

A Citroën club 'rendezvous' in the USA.

UK parts suppliers

Andrew Brodie Engineering
www.brodie.co.uk

Andy Spares
www.andyspares.com

Classic Citroën Parts
www.classic-citroen-parts.co.uk

John Greaves
www.citroenspecialists.com

Pleiades
www.citroen-hydraulics.com

European parts suppliers
France
A A Garage
www.dspieces.com

DS Garage
www.dsgarage.com

Philippe Losson Citroën
www.losson.com

Retro Stock
Tel: 01 48 35 35 36

Germany
Dirk Sassen DS
www.ds-sassen.de

The Netherlands
Chyparse
Stemerdingweg 11,
3769 CE Soesterberg
Tel: 31 (0346) 351150

Citroën Andre
www.citroen-andre.com

Citron Pieces
www.citronpieces.com

Citrotech
www.citrotech.nl

CTA Service
www.ctaservice.nl

Blikwerk is a world-renowned restorer
located in The Netherlands.

USA parts suppliers
Brad Nauss Automotive
www.bradnaussauto.com

Shop Citroën
www.shopcitroen.com
e-mail: citroenconcours@yahoo.com

Western Hemispheres
www.westernhemispheres.com

UK specialists
Andrew Brodie Engineering
www.brodie.co.uk

Centreville Citroën
http://home2.btconnect.com/centreville/
index.html

DS World
www.dsworldltd.com/index.html

French Classics
www.frenchclassics.co.uk

John Greaves
www.citroenspecialists.com

European specialists
France
Philippe Losson Citroën
www.losson.com

Germany
Dirk Sassen DS
www.ds-sassen.de

The Netherlands
Blikwerk
www.blikwerk.nl

Citroën Andre
www.citroen-andre.com

Overseas specialists
Australia
AutoFrance
6 Lambs Rd, Artarmon 2064

Canada
Marc's Auto Repair
5542 Mavis St, Burnaby, BC

USA
Citroën Concours of America, Inc
San Diego, CA, USA
www.citroen-ca.com
e-mail: citroenconcours@yahoo.com

Dave Burnham Citroën
Delanson, NY, USA
e-mail: racing48@nycap.rr.com

Well-known DS Enthusiasts
Australia
Lloyd Sharp's Citroën Site
www.citroen.cc

Canada
Blair Anderson's Citroën Connection
www.citroen.mb.ca

A variety of D-models belonging to a
Belgian enthusiast.

The Netherlands
Toine Moors Website
www.toi.dds.nl/ds.html

UK
Julian Marsh's Citroenet
www.citroenet.org.uk

Citroën DS Books
Original Citroën DS
– John Reynolds
ISBN 10: 076032901X

Citroën DS Design Icon
– Malcolm Bobbitt
ISBN 13: 978-1-904788-30-0

Citroën DS and ID Gold Portfolio
– R M Clarke (compiler)
ISBN 10: 1855202255

Citroën DS The Complete Story
– John Pressnell
ISBN 10: 1861260555

La Citroën DS de mon pere (French)
– D Pagneux, ETAI.

Citroën DS 50 Ans de Passion
(French)
– Thibaut Amant, ETAI.

Numbers built
A total of 1,330,775 D-models were built worldwide between 1955 and 1975 – 783,863 of these were the 'series 2' version built after October 1965. The following are the major changes on the 'series 2' cars.

Production modifications
1966: A new 5-main-bearing engine replaces the ageing 11CV-derived 3-main bearing engine – along with the new engine, the D-model gets a new transmission, front brakes, driveshafts and 5-stud wheels (replacing the single-nut wheel):
– ID19 Berline: 1911cc, 74hp (DIN), top speed: 158km/h.
– ID19 Break: 1985cc, 74hp (DIN), top speed: 165km/h.
– ID21 Break: 2175cc, 100hp (DIN), top speed: 175km/h.
– DS19 Berline, Pallas and Prestige: 1985cc, 74hp (DIN), top speed: 165km/h.
– DS21 Berline, Pallas, Prestige and Cabriolet: 2175cc, 100hp (DIN), top speed:175km/h.

1967: All models get mineral oil for their hydraulic system – this excluded any cars built for North America, which were awaiting DOT (Department of Transportation) approval to use the mineral-based LHM fluid in the braking system. Because of the fluid's colour, this new system is referred to as the green system and the older vegetable-based LHS system is commonly referred to as the red system.
New engine for the ID19: 1985cc, 78hp (DIN), top speed: 160km/h.

1968: All models get glass-covered dual-headlight fenders. Also, standard on all DS models and an option on all other cars, the inner headlights, connected by an ingenious albeit simple mechanism of rods and cables to the steering, would pivot to allow the car's driver to see around a corner. USA-bound cars were again stymied by the DOT and instead received a less attractive, coverless, sealed-beam, lighting system mounted in painted aluminium housings.

1969: Power boosts for most engines, new dashboard with squared-off buttons (replacing the round buttons of earlier years), a large turning wheel now controls seat reclining. In mid-1969, the DOT finally approves the LHM fluid and all USA models are now sold with the green system hydraulics.
– ID19 Berline: 1985cc, 81.5hp (DIN), top speed: 160km/h.
– ID20 Berline: 1985cc, 91hp (DIN), top speed: 167km/h.
– DS20 Berline: 1985cc, 91hp (DIN), top speed: 167km/h.
– DS21 Berline: 2175cc, 106hp (DIN), top speed: 178km/h.
– Breaks: 20 and 21 engines.

1970: The ID19 is replaced by the D Spèciale, and the ID20 is replaced by the D Super. All cars get a new dashboard with three round dials including a rev counter. The newest family member is the DS21 EFi – the first French produced car to offer electronic fuel injection. 2175cc, 125hp (DIN), top speed: 188km/h.

1971: Last year for the DS cabriolet. The DS21 Prestige is replaced by the DS21 Prestige Pallas. A 5-speed gearbox is introduced and is standard on the DS21 but optional on other cars. Interestingly, the USA market, which continues to import the D-model until 1972, is never offered the 5-speed gearbox – not even as an option.

1972: The swivelling self-levelling headlights are now standard on all but the D Super models (which offer it as an option). Extruded push-button door handles are replaced with recessed lift handles. Minor upgrades included a plastic-over-foam-covered steering wheel and standard air horns. Major new options include air conditioning with front bumper air intakes and a fully automatic Borg Warner gearbox.
    The DS20 gets a 5hp engine upgrade: 99hp (DIN), top speed: 169km/h.

1973: A new DS, the D Super 5 with the 2175cc, 106hp (DIN) engine from the DS21 and a 5-speed gearbox – but with lower trim level than the DS21. The DS21 is replaced by the DS23 – which is sold in both carburetted and electronic injection versions and three gearbox possibilities: Citromatic, 5-speed manual or Borg Warner full automatic.
– DS23, Carb, 2347cc, 115hp (DIN), top speed: 179km/h.
– DS23 EFi, 2347cc, 130hp (DIN), top speed: 188km/h.
The D Spècial gets the 99hp (DIN) engine from the D Super.

1974: Virtually no change as Citroën winds down model production in anticipation of its replacement, the CX.

1975: April 24, the 1,330,775[th] and final DS rolls of the production line.

Common mechanical details
Front-wheel drive
Engine: Water-cooled pushrod OHV four-in-line cylinders with cast-iron block and alloy hemispherical cylinder head.
Transmission: Mounted in front of engine – Manual: side column shift with either four or five forward gears and synchromesh on all but the first. Citromatic: top column shift with four forward gears and synchromesh on all but the first. Automatic: top column shift with Borg Warner three-speed full.
Brakes: Front inboard-mounted disc brakes with separate emergency pads, rear drum brakes.
Suspension: Front: twin leading suspension arms with anti-roll bar and self-levelling hydraulic suspension. Rear: trailing arms with anti-roll bar and self-levelling hydraulic suspension.
Steering: Rack and pinion – either hydraulically assisted or manual.
Electricals: 12-volt negative ground battery.

Serial numbers
To view serial numbers for 1966-1975 D models, as well as post publication news, updates and amendments relating to this book please visit www.veloce.co.uk/book/V4138

The Essential Buyer's Guide™ series ...

978-1-845840-22-8

978-1-845840-26-6

978-1-845840-29-7

978-1-845840-77-8

978-1-845840-99-0

978-1-904788-70-6

978-1-845841-01-0

978-1-845841-19-5

978-1-845841-13-3

978-1-845841-35-5

978-1-845841-36-2

978-1-845841-38-6

978-1-845841-46-1

978-1-845841-47-8

978-1-845841-63-8

978-1-845841-65-2

978-1-845841-88-1

978-1-845841-92-8

978-1-845842-00-0

978-1-845842-04-8

978-1-845842-05-5

978-1-845842-70-3

978-1-845842-81-9

978-1-845842-83-3

978-1-845842-84-0

978-1-845842-87-1

978-1-84584-134-8

978-1-845843-03-8

978-1-845843-09-0

978-1-845843-16-8

978-1-845843-29-8

978-1-845843-30-4

978-1-845843-34-2

978-1-845843-38-0

978-1-845843-39-7

978-1-845841-61-4

978-1-845842-31-4

978-1-845843-07-6

978-1-845843-40-3

978-1-845843-48-9

978-1-845843-63-2

978-1-845844-09-7